W9-ALW-061

NOV 1 1 2003

OPPORTUNITIES

in

Interior Design and Decorating Careers

OPPORTUNITIES

in

Interior Design and Decorating Careers

REVISED EDITION

DAVID STEARNS

ROUND LAKE AREA
LIBRARY
906 HART ROAD
ROUND LAKE, IL 60073
(847) 546-7060

Mc
Graw
Hill

New York   Chicago   San Francisco   Lisbon   London   Madrid   Mexico City
Milan   New Delhi   San Juan   Seoul   Singapore   Sydney   Toronto

The *McGraw·Hill* Companies

Library of Congress Cataloging-in-Publication Data

Stearns, David.
    Opportunities in interior design and decorating careers / by David Stearns.
  —3rd ed.
       p.   cm.
    Includes bibliographical references.
    ISBN 13: 978-0-07-154532-7 (alk. paper)
    ISBN 10: 0-07-154532-8 (alk. paper)
    1. Interior decoration—Vocational guidance—United States.   I. Ball, Victoria
Kloss. Opportunities in interior design and decorating careers.   II. Title.

    NK2116.B3   2008
    747.023—dc22   2008024642

Copyright © 2009 by The McGraw-Hill Companies, Inc. All rights reserved. Printed in the
United States of America. Except as permitted under the United States Copyright Act of
1976, no part of this publication may be reproduced or distributed in any form or by
any means, or stored in a database or retrieval system, without the prior written
permission of the publisher.

1 2 3 4 5 6 7 8 9 10 11 12 13 14 15 16 17 18 19 20   DOC/DOC   0 9 8

ISBN 978-0-07-154532-7
MHID   0-07-154532-8

Interior design by Rattray Design

McGraw-Hill books are available at special quantity discounts to use as premiums and
sales promotions or for use in corporate training programs. To contact a representative,
please visit the Contact Us pages at www.mhprofessional.com.

This book is printed on acid-free paper.

Contents

ACKNOWLEDGMENTS

THIS BOOK IS of necessity indebted to the entire interior design profession for its material. We hope that all aspects of the profession have been given adequate, accurate, and appropriate coverage. It must be made clear, however, that the author accepts responsibility for all statements made herein.

1

WHAT IS INTERIOR DESIGN?

MOST OF US are familiar with the term *interior decorator*. We probably envision someone with an artistic eye who is hired to help customers select furnishings, wall coverings, and color schemes for their homes. We may even have formed our opinions based on what we see on television, from the designers of "Trading Spaces" to the complete reconstructions done by the range of designers on "Extreme Home Makeover."

Although achieving a pleasing decorating scheme is part of it, interior designers are professionals whose job is to plan and provide for the insides of buildings in order to make them as functional, beautiful, and meaningful as possible. They are responsible for directing any work that is necessary to achieve this result.

Given the broad nature of interior design, it can be difficult to separate it from other careers dealing with similar issues. This may lead to planning both an academic program and a professional career. In an academic curriculum, training for interior design may be found in various departments, such as art, architecture, human ecology, and home economics. Following is a list of some career disciplines related to interior design that are in current catalogs.

- Environmental planning
- Space planning: regional and city
- Construction engineering
- Architecture
- Landscape architecture
- Interior design
- Ecology: the interrelation between humans and their environment
- Design as related to the home

Disciplines Within Interior Design

There are numerous wide-ranging disciplines within the career field of interior design, including the following:

Structure

Of materials, such as woods, fabrics, glass, synthetics, plastics, ceramics, stones, metals, colorants, finishes

Of elaborate artifacts, such as furniture, cabinets, walls, windows, doors

Of building equipment systems

Function

Performance of materials

Performance of equipment

Interior space utilization

Specialized Performance
Toxicity
Fire prevention
Safety
Air conditioning
Illumination

Special Group Needs
Age groups
The handicapped
The sick

Business
Business principles and procedures
Organizing and managing an interior design business
Knowledge of details of an interior design business:
    sources, estimates, specifications, ordering, receiving,
    installing, billing, cost-accounting

Computer Technology
For presentations
For data recall
For business management

Presentation Skills
Drafting, rendering, and model making
Photography
Designing with computers
Speaking

Craft Skills
Weaving
Carpentry

Social Skills
Working with people
Working for people

Promotional Skills
Writing and speaking
Organizational work

Professional Skills
Knowledge of and working under a professional code
Working with others in the same profession

Aesthetics
Designing of interior details
Interior space planning from the visual point of view
Color and light planning in relation to space
Color and light, art and science interrelations—used for
    effective lighting and paint technology
Texture planning

Academic Disciplines with Cultural Implications
Economics
History
Language
Literature
Mathematics

Psychology
Physical sciences
Sociology

A Science or an Art?

The preceding lists show that interior design encompasses an understanding of many disciplines, which raises a question: is interior design a science or an art? In truth, it is both. Like most subjects today, interior design involves scientific material. It not only includes some matters of pure science, such as those found in the study of color and illumination, but also a vast amount of information that could be classified as applied science or technology, such as computer drafting.

Interior design is likewise an art—one of the more complex and perhaps more important fields of art. Just think of how much space it occupies in our art museums.

Because of this dual nature, interior design is a challenging subject that appeals to people who enjoy life in both scientific and aesthetic realms.

Interior Design as a Science

In both pure and applied science, the method employed to gain a result involves precise knowledge. This means that the facts of science can be taught and its dictates must be followed to solve many objective problems.

For instance, an architect must master the knowledge of how to construct a building so that it will stand, bear its load, enclose a satisfactory climate, and provide adequate illumination. Such structural knowledge likewise relates to the interior of a building. For example, the interior designer must know which walls are load-bearing, since they must not be destroyed unless there are reinforcements to compensate. How much weight can a partition support? What is the relation between any change in the design of a fireplace and its performance?

Because the equipment used in building and design is now fairly standardized, interior design has become a growing technological subject. For example, consider the technological aspect of space planning. We know the space required by a person walking or by groups engaged in conversation. We know the standardized sizes of kitchen and bath equipment, storage space, and comfortable space for dining.

More than that, scientists can measure some of the psychological aspects of space; for instance, how much is required for psychological ease, at what point claustrophobia begins to set in, and when space is so vast that it loses its human quality. If these seem like frivolous considerations, think about your own comfort level in various situations. Are you comfortable in your bedroom: is there enough room to sleep, read, and use a computer? Or do you feel hemmed in by a small space and crave more room for your needs? Anyone who has ever shared a room with a sibling or lived in a dorm with a roommate may well be able to understand this.

Taken to the next step, we can project some of this objective knowledge about space into phases of interior design that are growing in popularity. Is there any change in space demands for the elderly, for the sick, or for the child at school?

Some disciplines exist in the border territory between art and science, such as marketing. For example, a designer must understand price in the market and the economic theories that govern it in order to have a successful career.

There is so much that a qualified interior designer should know that falls under the heading of science that you may wonder whether we have forgotten that the subject of interior design is, more important, an art.

Interior Design as an Art

As we mentioned, there can be a tendency to forget that interior design is an important art. It is more than a core of disciplines that can be routinely taught and easily learned. Let's talk a bit about art in general to gain an understanding of how it applies to interior design.

First, the materials and organization of art are basic to life. Art is a manipulation of the ingredients of life—usually sensuous material because the senses are avenues for the entrance of life—to move people emotionally and often intellectually, to help them see life in new ways. Their sensations and their thoughts are changed in the process; art is the organization of details in order to achieve such aesthetic stimulation.

Second, the response to art is individual. People view art with their own eyes, never with yours or anyone else's. You've probably heard the expression, "I don't know art, but I know what I like." This is true for many people who have a sense of what they find appealing without having a full understanding of the artistic process or the differences in art styles. In many cases, the more art people are exposed to, the more they will find to like. Art can change people because it changes their perceptions.

Similarly, people can grow in an appreciation of art. Good art is always what we choose to call beautiful. When you have created art, it is not certain that everyone will immediately recognize it. But beauty in and of itself creates sensitivity; it creates an avenue for growing appreciation.

Beauty in interior design carries the idea of an emotional pleasure that joins the mind and the senses in a form that is directly related to use. This brings up the question of taste, because what may seem to be the right solution to one person may not appeal to another. The interaction among art, designer, and patron is a difficult consideration for all the environmental arts. Since interior design deals with environments that lie close to people, it is important for the designer to avoid assuming that only he or she has the right solution.

A workable professional interior design solution must include a reciprocity between client and designer that produces an answer that both parties find pleasing. This is not necessarily in the nature of a compromise, which may please neither; it is a solution that will give each satisfaction.

A Final Thought

This discussion about the science and art of interior design is presented for one reason: to lead you to an understanding of the importance of choosing a good school with a solid academic program that will teach you the entire scope of the profession. It is important to learn the lessons of both good science and good art and to understand how they come together in good interior design.

2

Nature of Interior Design

JUST AS INTERIOR design may be defined as both a science and an art, it can also be considered a business and a profession. Although they seem similar, the two terms do have differences, which we will consider in this chapter.

A Business and a Profession

It often has been facetiously said that a job is work for pay while a career is trained work engaged in for an appreciable period of time for compensation—once you boil down the second definition, it's really the same as the first. Business is buying and selling for the best possible monetary profit, while a profession provides a worthwhile service requiring much knowledge at a reward fixed by ethical considerations. Although these last two definitions are fairly accurate, the bottom line need not be the only consideration in business nor the altruistic motive necessarily the only controlling factor in a profession. Your sense of values can enable the two to join in partnership.

It's important to remember, however, that careers and classifications can change. The first essential qualification for a career to be a profession is that its practicing members should adhere to educational standards and to an ethical way of conducting their business.

First, let's consider the definition of the professional interior designer as endorsed by its largest professional organization, the American Society of Interior Designers:

> Interior design includes a scope of services performed by a professional design practitioner, qualified by means of education, experience, and examinations, to protect and enhance the life, health, safety, and welfare of the public. These services may include any or all of the following tasks:
>
> - Research and analysis of the client's goals and requirements; and development of documents, drawings, and diagrams that outline those needs
> - Formulation of preliminary space plans and two- and three-dimensional design concept studies and sketches that integrate the client's program needs and are based on knowledge of the principles of interior design and theories of human behavior
> - Confirmation that preliminary space plans and design concepts are safe, functional, aesthetically appropriate, and meet all public health, safety and welfare requirements, including code, accessibility, environmental, and sustainability guidelines
> - Selection of colors, materials, and finishes to appropriately convey the design concept and to meet socio-psychological, functional, maintenance, life-cycle performance, environmental, and safety requirements
> - Selection and specification of furniture, fixtures, equipment and millwork, including layout drawings and detailed prod-

uct description; and provision of contract documentation to facilitate pricing, procurement, and installation of furniture
- Provision of project management services, including preparation of project budgets and schedules
- Preparation of construction documents, consisting of plans, elevations, details, and specifications to illustrate nonstructural and/or nonseismic partition layouts; power and communications locations; reflected ceiling plans and lighting design; materials and finishes; and furniture layouts
- Coordination and collaboration with other allied design professionals who may be retained to provide consulting services, including but not limited to architects; structural, mechanical, and electrical engineers; and various specialty consultants
- Confirmation that construction documents for nonstructural and/or nonseismic construction are signed and sealed by the responsible interior designer, as applicable to jurisdictional requirements for filing with code enforcement officials
- Administration of contract documents, bids, and negotiations as the client's agent
- Observation and reporting on the implementation of projects while in progress and upon completion, as a representative of and on behalf of the client; and conducting postoccupancy evaluation reports

A large portion of interior design is in the contract field where the standardization of products makes it possible to subcontract work, so that interior designers may send some of the specified work out to freelancers. In some cases, however, subcontracting is not feasible because the client wants the designer to keep very close supervision over the project.

Two additional factors prevent interior design from being considered solely a large-quantity piece of production. First, since the work involves designing an indoor environment for individuals, there are times when a standardized solution will not suffice. Second, it is nearly impossible to write specifications for particular high-end items. For example, what subcontractor could handle an order for Van Gogh's *Sunflowers* or for an eighteenth-century Kerman oriental carpet? Artistic creativity does not necessarily fit into neat patterns.

A professional person must conduct business in a way that is consistent with the ethical stipulations of his or her professional group. But it's important to note that not all professional groups can adopt the same rules and regulations relative to their operation because not all activities, even within the same profession, are equivalent. For instance, a doctor who delivers a baby may have an hourly fee, a family physician may charge a fixed amount per examination, and a dentist may go up and down the price ladder according to the cost of materials.

What is important is that the participating parties know and agree to the manner of payment and that the work is honestly carried out according to the terms of the agreement.

So, with this in mind, we can say that interior design may be regarded either as a business conducted in a professional manner or as a profession conducted in an ethical business manner.

Beginning a Project

Interior design has changed a great deal over the past thirty years. Today it operates on a much larger scale than in the past, and it is concerned with a broader spectrum of activities, so its organizational units are frequently much larger. Although many interior design companies are very large, this doesn't mean that a small company with no more than five designers on its staff—or even a one-person business—is a thing of the past. In a small company or individual practice, many more opportunities may exist for more personalized relations. We'll begin with a small enterprise as our model, and in later chapters we'll discuss how other situations differ from this.

What does an interior designer do on a job? Let's say that you are a newly trained graduate who has just been hired at a small firm. The first few months of any career should provide the opportunity to observe all the facets of the company. Among these, of course, is the opportunity to do some designing, but don't rush this phase of the work until you are certain that you have a clear understanding of the details of procedure.

Let's assume that the firm that employs you works primarily with individual private clients. Many small firms or individuals going into private practice are not geared to designing for large contracts, so their customers are individuals rather than corporations.

Your first assignment will usually involve a talk with your client. But how did you get the client? Your superiors may have decided to let you try your hand, so they have assigned you to one of their less-complicated jobs. Perhaps you have done some work that has been noticed and your services have been requested, or maybe the client has met and liked you.

Your client may have confidence in you as a person. This confidence factor is important in all client decisions, and it is probably a valid reason for choosing one designer over another. And it is certainly built right into the success of a piece of work: if there is no confidence between designer and client, by definition there will be no success, because both designer and client must value the finished design for it to be good.

In any firm, however small, you should have a work space. For an interior designer who is sensitive to the environment, this private area, often no more than a desk, is important and should be made as pleasant as possible. The headquarters of an interior design firm is frequently located outside of the high-rent district. However, the location must be attractive, easily accessible, safe, and not without a certain kind of prestige of its own. The need to keep overhead costs to a minimum often makes it difficult to locate in a prestigious spot. With smaller space allowed for the entire firm, you, too, will have to learn to be a good space organizer and to make your station attractive on a shoestring budget.

Now you find yourself facing someone who seeks the expertise that you feel capable of providing. Your first obligation is to try to interview the prospective client in order to understand and interpret his or her wants and needs. This may take skillful effort on your part, because some people scarcely know their own wants and needs except in the most general terms. They may talk about wanting to brighten up their living room without giving you any real idea of how they use the space, or they may mention a place to entertain and leave you up in the air as to whether they enjoy formal dinner parties or informal gatherings.

Use this initial conference to gain an idea of the scope of the work. Then you may mention some similar jobs you or your firm have completed. For a really large project, the client may wish to interview several firms before making a decision. If your firm was recommended due to previous work, you may stand a very good chance of winning the job.

Whatever else occurs, this first interview should establish rapport between you and the client. If it does not, then it is possible that something is fundamentally wrong—you or your firm may not be just the right partner for the undertaking. It is better to chalk up the interview to experience before any damage is done.

End your initial conference decisively and graciously. Hours are worth money, and by this time you should have a preliminary understanding of the client's ideas and needs and will have agreed to prepare a proposal to meet the requirements.

At this stage or after a second meeting, you and the client will proceed with the project. Usually at this second meeting you will suggest an approximate budget for the project, including a guarantee that you will receive a certain percentage of that cost, whether or not the project is accepted for completion. This guarantee is a safeguard to protect your most valuable asset as a designer: your ideas. The guarantee differs from project to project and depends on company policy.

Programming

Compiling and organizing the data related to a project is called *programming*. The first step is often to secure information on the location, which can be in the form of an architectural plan or computer image. Three-dimensional computer images can aid in your understanding of unconstructed space. If the project also involves an architect or other professional, such as a lighting engineer, it may be necessary to confer with that person, also.

You certainly will want to visit the site. In working as a visual artist within a prescribed architectural framework, it is essential to fix this framework in both your visual and psychological memory. There may be aspects of the situation that only become apparent when you are on location, and a visit may give you a better psychological perspective from which to work.

You must verify the measurements for key positions. If any furnishings don't fit, possibly because some changes were made on a later set of plans that you have not received, you are nevertheless the one who is held responsible.

Once you have a firm picture of your assignment, you are ready to begin planning one or more solutions. Think through the problem until you arrive at what seems to you to be the most satisfactory answer. Then plan a second, perhaps less expensive, alternative.

The number of presentations should not be too many, however. In the first place, too many options will simply confuse both you and your client. This does not mean that some alterations can't be made later, but even these should be held to a minimum in order to avoid a resulting uncoordinated scheme that has none of the virtues of the original.

The real reason for not making and presenting too many proposals is the fact that as an artist, the more you ponder the matter the more certainly one plan will assert itself as the right one. Artists generally have firm convictions about their work, and they don't easily give up their ideas.

Here, of course, is a paradox. As an interior designer, you are not a starving artist willing to give up all for your art. Quite the contrary, yours is a social art, and you will often have to find a way to persuade a skeptical client that your plan is the best solution.

The presentation to your client usually includes scaled floor plans with descriptions of any changes in lighting, fenestration (window arrangement), or permanent fixtures. Color charts, photographs of furnishings, and samples of materials for furniture, floor coverings, and window treatments are required. In many cases you will also prepare color renderings or three-dimensional computer images. If the job includes custom-designed furnishings, preliminary drawings must be presented. Each project will be unique with respect to the total amount of illustrative material required and warranted.

The aim of the second client conference should be to get approval and acceptance for one plan. Once this is accomplished, you will send the client a written estimate of the costs involved; the estimate will later be carefully itemized. Preparing the estimate will involve your knowledge of the management and business disciplines previously mentioned.

If this proposal meets with the client's approval, a contract will be written and presented. This is a legal agreement between your firm and the client. The contract usually includes a fee-payment schedule. Because a great amount of time, money, and purchases are involved in completing the project, it is customarily paid for as the work progresses, with a residual amount due on its completion.

After the contract is accepted, you will begin placing orders for materials, scheduling work, supervising quality, and keeping the project running smoothly. Only when the customer is satisfied may the project be properly considered to be completed. As you can see, you are now calling upon other skills in addition to your artistry, such as negotiation, time management, and supervision.

In some ways this scenario is typical, but in others it is not. Many projects are simpler, and many are far more complicated, requiring many meetings, much consultation, elaborate plans, and copious cost sheets.

Maintaining Client Relationships

Many interior designers are able to maintain long-term alliances with clients, brought about by warmhearted relations and good service. This type of association is particularly characteristic of interior design work for individual clients. A good deal of private practice, especially in residential work, is apt to be a continuing process. Certain people speak of their designer in much the same way they would of their attorney; a satisfied client doesn't shop around or change.

Many people purchase older homes, particularly in an uncertain real estate market when newer dwellings are more expensive. Let's suppose that a family has just moved to a new city, and they have bought a home because the schools, church, and civic facilities desired are nearby. The house needs reconditioning—the walls must be brought back to prime, and the floors need to be refinished. The house must be made sound before it is refurnished. It may even need serious mechanical work, such as renovating the entire sanitary, heating, and electrical systems. Perhaps the exterior must be made watertight before extensive interior repairs can begin.

A professional interior designer should advise this client on the order of procedure and whom to call for operations. The designer may be equipped to subcontract some of the work, such as exterior painting or interior flooring. In any case, the interior designer's opinion is valuable in such situations.

In other situations, there may be occasional crises to be met, and often there is a perpetual schedule of protective and remedial care. For instance, a client may have a sofa that needs recovering this year or a bedroom that needs renovation the next; perhaps the requirement is for a rug to place in a hall. It is important that the client be able to call on someone who has the overall picture in mind and who is competent to suggest something new that harmonizes with the old. This in the long run saves money for the client.

This kind of continuous planning is not limited to designing for houses, and it is a large-scale operation for some design firms. After the initial installation, say in a commercial project, the firm may contract to keep the interiors in both visual and physical repair. This sort of arrangement assures the occupants that their investment will be well maintained.

Another type of long-term designing contract is made with the owner of a building in which spaces are leased to individual tenants. This could involve an apartment building, an office complex, a shopping mall, or a condominium. The lessee is placed under obligation to give all designing commissions to the designated firm, which assures the other tenants of a qualified grade of work throughout, which protects their own equity.

Such a contract also safeguards the building's owner. For example, the designer may be asked to alter a space that has been used by a men's clothing store so that it will be suitable for a bookshop. The client who has moved into an apartment may want two suites made into one or want changes in walls, doors, or lighting. It is important to the owner of the building to know that the work be done by someone who knows how to proceed safely and correctly.

When this owner-renter policy carries into large contract work, it may require the services of an architecture and interior design firm for any remodeling. This arrangement has many advantages, provided full scope and appreciation are given to the potential of each profession. This will be further detailed in Chapter 6, Custom and Contract Designing.

Many interior designers are particularly gratified by long-term relationships with clients. The regard of a customer for the interior designer is usually quite genuine. It is a close and trusting relationship that results from helping others design their immediate environment. The real reward comes from being able to serve the practical and psychological needs of clients, so that your solution will give them pleasure.

Types of Specialized Interiors

The types of interiors that you will handle as a designer are limited only by your ability to recognize a specialized need. When a project involves equipping a building for its specialized function, an interior designer is the professional who can provide results.

Although many firms are unable to specialize too narrowly, there are some fascinating areas that require considerable knowledge and skill. For example, designers are hired to work with seacraft, aircraft, ski lodges, and vacation resorts. Schools, churches, hospitals, and stores present their own unique problems. Other specialties include designing of accommodations for older citizens, day-care facilities, accommodations for the handicapped—the list is as long as the growing number of specializations in modern life.

Even prison facilities need interior design. This is not necessarily to pamper the inmates, but it is more concerned with factors of safety, humanity, and environmental awareness. In any setting, the interior designer requires imagination to see the need, the talent and skill to prepare a solution, and the sense to see whether an idea is practical.

Methods of Receiving Payment

In addition to your aesthetic aspirations, you have also entered into your career as a preferred way of earning a living. As an interior designer, you may legitimately earn this livelihood in one of several ways. These depend on the nature of the task; in a complex job, several of them or a modification of one of them may be used. Each method is professionally recognized as legitimate, provided it is suited to the operation and agreed upon by the participants.

Fixed Fee

Some designers work on a fixed-fee basis. This method is particularly applicable when clients prefer to do their own purchasing. The fee must reflect the time and skill spent in advising and in writing specifications for particular products.

Contract business is often conducted on a fee basis. The design firm might plan the interiors and supply carefully detailed specs. In very large-volume business, the client may prefer to do his or her own ordering, if sources of supplies are available.

Consultation Method

If the job doesn't include writing specifications, the consultation method of payment may be used. For example, this might apply when a school board wishes to make its own selections and place its own contracts but wants professional advice in the planning.

Salary

Designing can also be done on a strict salary basis. Large companies or syndicates, the government, architectural firms, and many interior design firms often employ interior designers on that basis.

Retail-Wholesale Differential

Some designing service is negotiated on the basis of the difference between wholesale and retail prices. This method may be most suited to smaller projects where it may prove most understandable and convenient for the client. Or it could be used for a certain portion of the work if the client wants the designer to take full charge.

Your training will include courses in how to conduct business professionally. Each job presents its own requirements; in the final analysis, you should use whichever method best suits the specific situation. In a professional undertaking, the basis of charging must be clearly stated according to the best business principles; it must be understood by both designer and client, and it must be conscientiously carried out.

Custom Designing

Interior designers sometimes incur additional costs when they act as custom designers. Most major installations call for some type of custom designing, such as a mural to be painted, a light fixture to be designed, built-in furniture to be constructed, or a rug to be woven. In such cases the designer acts in the capacity of industrial designer and charges accordingly.

The money comes, of course, from the client and must reflect the creative talent, the required labor, and the capital involved. Management keeps these factors under control, and professional ethics keeps them equitable.

Types of Interior Design Firms

An interior design firm may be established in several ways: as an individually owned firm, a partnership, a corporation, or a combined business with architecture services or an architectural firm.

Before making a final decision about which structure to choose, it is important to consider all relevant factors, such as financial status, long-term goals, and business experience. It is also a good idea to consult an accountant and attorney who are knowledgeable in business matters. Let's consider the advantages and drawbacks of these different organizational structures.

Individually Owned Firms

Some designers set up independent firms, although it is generally best to gain experience in an established company before taking this step.

What will you need to run your own business? First, a professional designer must have a place of business, even if it is only one room at home reserved exclusively for this purpose.

Then there is the need for capital, generally computed as at least the advance of six months' expenses. You will need this money in order to purchase samples and supplies, to meet labor costs, to set up office procedures and equipment, and to establish credit.

An individually owned establishment has the obvious advantage of placing all control in your own hands, a precious boon if you happen to be a person with decided opinions about aesthetics.

However, an individually owned firm is one of the most risky, for there is no sharing of expenses if mistakes are made. The individual owner is held legally responsible for any financial losses incurred by the business.

Partnerships

Being a member of a partnership may be a distinct advantage for the designer. Not only are expenses divided, but it often is possible to gain a partner who, though with similar talents in many ways, could be a complement in others. One partner might know artistry; the other could be the business expert. The benefits are obvious.

The drawback of a partnership is that each partner may be held legally responsible for the debts of the business, including those caused by other partners. Choosing a partner should be done with great care.

Corporations

A corporation resembles a partnership in that the people who establish it share the initial expenses and eventual profits. But once established, a corporation is considered an entity unto itself; the founders personally are not legally liable for the company's debts.

This fact reduces some of the risk associated with an individually owned business or a partnership. However, the more complex laws governing corporations may sometimes dissuade people from choosing this organizational structure.

Architectural–Interior Design Firms

A growing number of firms are organized with both architects and interior designers as owners and are thus equipped to offer both types of professional services. This sort of firm differs from one that is predominantly an architectural firm that hires interior designers to handle interior designing. In the cooperatively owned firm (frequently a family organization), both professions can practice independently, calling upon each other as needed.

The number of architectural–interior design firms is growing due to the recognition that skilled interior designers have additional expertise that may contribute to the firm's overall effectiveness and success.

It is important to remember, however, that in joining such a firm or any specialized firm for that matter, you may find the work somewhat prescribed by the overall type of design for which the firm is known.

Tools of the Trade

The interior designer advises clients about a number of individual pieces of interior furnishing. In most cases the designer must also be able to locate these items. One of your most valuable professional assets—probably ranking next to artistic ability—will be your knowledge of the quality of supplies and of the sources from which they may be acquired. Supplies can be anything from furniture to pictures to fabrics to floor coverings. Where do these items come from, and how can one person know about them all?

Standard items, such as cabinet hardware, come from a wholesaler and can be ordered by item number. For a less common item, you may examine the run of the merchandise (often known as the *line*), perhaps by using manufacturers' catalogs. Most prominent suppliers maintain show space in what is generally known as a *design center*, where they exhibit the best of their current offerings. These showrooms are usually off-limits to the general public because they are for the wholesale trade, but some are open to the public, with merchandise displayed at retail prices.

The largest design center is the Merchandise Mart in Chicago, a twenty-five-story building that includes 4.2 million gross square feet over two city blocks. Other excellent marts are located throughout the United States and Canada.

Although these marts run continual displays, they set aside several weeks in the spring and fall for presenting new products. This is when many designers visit them, as they present an opportunity both to appraise the offerings and to attend the many special lectures given at those times. In addition individual niches of the design industry have their own special shows timed. For instance, the furniture industry, which is concentrated in North Carolina, holds its annual market every spring.

These occasions aren't all drudgery, especially not for those who enjoy the camaraderie of meeting colleagues from different locations. The marts present an excellent opportunity for designers to learn what is new in the industry and to make valuable contacts with others in the trade.

In addition to the general furnishing mart, a designer must know all the reputable sources where unique quality accessories and fine art may be found. When these objects are second-rate, the entire character of a design may be lost.

Collaborating with Skilled Craft Workers

Working as a designer will mean that you have to know as much as possible about furnishings of all types. It also means that you'll need to know where to find the professionals who can create and install these items. Custom draperies, upholstery, wall coverings, and finishes must be expertly done. The designer should know standards of excellence, how these standards are measured, and expect the best service from the skilled craft workers hired.

Every designer also needs a place where orders may be received and inspected before they are detailed to a client. Some large design firms maintain their own workshops and allow other designers to subcontract work through their staff. Primary workshops generally also serve as warehouses. Most workshops are divided into departments, such as one for woodworking, one for textile handling, and one for work with paint and wall finishes.

Whether a designer chooses to subcontract work or to hire independent firms and craft workers, it is ultimately the designer's responsibility to employ workers who are fully competent for the job. This is one of the designer's most important commitments.

Human Factors

Since interior design is a social art (and business), you will find that a good deal of your time is spent in contact with other people. This can be a very pleasant aspect of your career, particularly since you will be interacting with many like-minded professionals. Not every artisan you encounter will be your type of person, of course, but you will most likely meet others who share your values and professional ethics.

You will meet people with highly individualized interests, purposes, abilities, and character—some may even be a bit eccentric. Many designers have aesthetic sensitivities and yet are practical and down-to-earth in demonstrating them. Some are decidedly conventional in their tastes; others are more modern and innovative.

Interior designers are usually alert to what is happening in the world, sensitive to changing trends and current events. If you choose wisely, you should find that you will be spending your days working with interior designers who will become your friends.

Your suppliers may also share some of these same characteristics. A good supplier is an important part of merchandising, which is a vital part of running your business. It is possible to establish a strong relationship with a supplier, based on an honest working relationship. Of course, you need to purchase the highest quality materials at the best possible prices, but if you can show loyalty to a supplier, you will generally be rewarded with discounts and excellent service. An experienced supplier can even teach you a great deal about your industry.

Whether you work for a large or small firm, you will interact with an office staff whose help may be invaluable. From the secretary who remembers that a client wants an order finished in time for a child's birthday to the purchasing assistant who always knows which suppliers offer the best prices, you will find some of your greatest allies among the administrative staff. It's important to remember the concept of teamwork and to show genuine appreciation for the work of these fellow professionals.

And last but not least, we shouldn't forget about the clients. Depending on the type of firm you work for and your specialization, your clients may come from a range of economic classes and cultural backgrounds. The basis for any relationship with a client will be the quality of your work and the kind of person you are.

A lot will depend on you and what you bring to these relationships with colleagues, suppliers, and clients. The interests that you cultivate through other sources, such as your church, club, volunteer work, and social groups, among many others, will affect who you are professionally.

Working Conditions

Regular working hours do exist in interior design, but don't expect them to be the norm. Because the work depends so heavily on other people, from clients to craft workers to suppliers, their schedules can't help but impact yours.

Even a newly hired designer will be expected to help out after normal business hours with details such as taking inventory, assisting with rush orders, and perhaps accompanying a senior designer on a weekend visit to a client.

Given the nature of the work, you will often face deadlines and may have to work long hours to meet them. There will occasionally be backorders in materials or the need to find a substitute for a discontinued item. And because the client is the boss, you'll have to schedule meetings at her or his convenience. In addition, the client might reject a proposed plan, and you'll have to start over.

Interior design was at one time a more seasonal business, the first rush being in the spring to coincide with the flurry of housecleaning followed by a second busy time before the winter holidays when clients prepared for entertaining. Vacations usually filled in the gaps. Today's schedule is largely unpredictable and depends on when a big contract comes onto the board. In this atmosphere vacations may be difficult to plan—they may coincide with a much needed rest, or they may come as a result of some lull in assignments.

Each studio has its own regulations about vacations. Customarily the so-called novice is entitled to a week's vacation with pay at the end of the first year on the job. Sometimes an extra week without pay may be arranged. The vacations, of course, grow longer and the salary higher as time progresses.

Sometimes the work itself affords a trip to a foreign destination or a vacation spot. Interior design contracts today are global, and in some situations travel may be considered a necessity, not only to attend conventions and accept assignments in foreign places but likewise for cultural purposes.

Earnings

Now the big question: what kind of salary can you expect to earn? Salaries vary depending on your level of education and experience, the type of employer, your geographic location, and your reputation or that of your firm.

Median annual earnings for wage and salary interior designers are about $42,260. The majority earn between $31,830 and $57,230, while the lowest 10 percent earn less than $24,270, and the highest 10 percent more than $78,760.

Median annual earnings in the industries employing the largest numbers of interior designers are:

Architectural, engineering, and related services	$46,750
Specialized design services	$43,250
Furniture stores	$38,980
Building material and supplies dealers	$36,650

Among salaried interior designers, those in large specialized design and architectural firms tend to earn higher and more stable salaries. Interior designers working in retail stores usually earn a commission, which may be irregular.

For residential design projects, self-employed interior designers and those working in smaller firms usually earn a per-hour consulting fee plus a percentage of the total cost of furniture, lighting, artwork, and other design elements. For commercial projects, they might charge a per-hour consulting fee, charge by the square footage, or charge a flat fee for the entire project. Also, designers who use specialty contractors usually earn a percentage of the contractor's earnings on the project in return for hiring the contractor. Self-employed designers must provide their own benefits.

3

Educational and Personal Requirements

At this point you understand that interior design is an art and a science, a business and a profession. You are familiar with some of the intricacies of interior design practice. So, what steps will you have to take in order to make this your career?

Once you are confident that this is the path you'd like to follow, you can start exploring the educational options that will prepare you for working as an interior designer.

High School Preparation

A high school diploma or its equivalent is customarily required for entrance to any school qualified to give the interior design training you will need for professional status.

If you are attending a technical high school, you might be able to take some courses in art or woodworking or fabric construction that will give you a taste for subjects that you'll encounter in your later education. The same advice applies if you are attending an academic high school, where a college preparatory program is available to students who plan to enter a four-year college or university.

Whatever your future plans, you should use your high school years to obtain a solid scholastic foundation. Training in the fundamentals of English is indispensable. With interior design rapidly becoming a global profession, it is also a good idea to study a foreign language. Mathematics is necessary for all sciences, and you should also include the study of history and political science.

Your social life and participation in sports are important, too. They will teach you about teamwork, leadership, and discipline and about how to get along with others.

Postsecondary Education

To be qualified for most entry-level positions in interior design, you will need postsecondary education, especially a bachelor's degree. You may find training programs at professional design schools or at colleges and universities; most usually take two to four years to complete. Graduates of two-year or three-year programs are awarded certificates or associate degrees in interior design and normally qualify as assistants to interior designers upon graduation. Graduates with a bachelor's degree usually qualify for a formal design apprenticeship program.

The National Association of Schools of Art and Design accredits approximately 250 postsecondary institutions with programs in art and design. Most of these schools award a degree in interior design. You may be required to submit sketches and other examples of your artistic ability, and once accepted, you will complete basic coursework, including computer-aided design (CAD), drawing, perspective, spatial planning, color and fabrics, furniture design, architecture, ergonomics, ethics, and psychology.

The National Council for Interior Design Qualification (NCIDQ) also accredits interior design programs in both the United States and Canada that lead to a bachelor's degree. There are currently 145 accredited bachelor's degree programs in interior design in the United States and 11 in Canada; most are part of schools or departments of art, architecture, or home economics.

A complete list of accredited programs is available at the council's website, www.accredit-id.org/accreditedprograms.

Apprenticeship

After completing your formal training, you will enter a one-year to three-year apprenticeship to gain experience before taking a licensing exam. Most apprentices work in design or architecture firms under the supervision of an experienced designer. You may also choose to gain experience working as an in-store designer in furniture stores.

The NCIDQ offers the Interior Design Experience Program (IDEP), which helps entry-level interior designers gain valuable supervised work experience and also offers mentoring services and workshops to new designers. It can provide a valuable transition between school and professional practice, as well as preparation for the NCIDQ examination and for licensure/registration.

Postgraduate Programs

Advanced programs generally require at least thirty credits for a master's degree and ninety credits for a doctorate. To be accepted into a graduate program, you will need to show evidence of your creative design ability in addition to your undergraduate record. Most programs include a thesis project based on academic research or creative design.

Licensure

Twenty-three states, the District of Columbia, Puerto Rico, and seven provinces register or license interior designers. The national council administers the licensing exam for interior design qualification. To be eligible to take the exam, you must have at least six years of combined education and experience in interior design, of which at least two years must be postsecondary education in design.

Once you have passed the qualifying exam, you will be granted the title of Certified, Registered, or Licensed Interior Designer, depending on the state or province. You will be obligated to complete continuing education credits in order to maintain licensure.

For information about the licensing exam, visit the NCIDQ website at www.ncidq.org/exam.

Certification and Advancement

You may obtain an optional certification in kitchen and bath design from the National Kitchen and Bath Association. The association offers three different levels of certification for kitchen and bath designers in the United States and Canada, each achieved through training seminars and certification exams. For complete information, go to www.nkba.org/education_certification.

As a beginning interior designer, you will receive on-the-job training and normally need one to three years of training before you can advance to higher-level positions. Employers increasingly prefer interior designers who are familiar with computer-aided design software and the basics of architecture and engineering to ensure that their designs meet building safety codes.

Membership in a professional association is one indication of an interior designer's qualifications and professional standing. The American Society of Interior Designers is the largest professional association for interior designers in North America, with forty-eight chapters throughout the United States and Canada. You may qualify for membership with at least a two-year degree and work experience. Professional organizations will be discussed in more detail in Chapter 8.

Experienced designers in large firms may advance to chief designer, design department head, or some other supervisory position. Some experienced designers open their own firms or decide to specialize in one aspect of interior design. Other designers leave the occupation to become teachers in schools of design or in colleges or universities. Many faculty members continue to consult privately or operate small design studios to complement their classroom activities.

Your Personal Qualifications

In addition to possessing technical knowledge, you must also be creative, imaginative, and persistent in order to succeed as an interior designer. You must also be able to communicate your ideas visually, verbally, and in writing. Because tastes in style can change quickly, you should be well read, open to new ideas and influences, and quick to react to changing trends.

Problem-solving skills and the ability to work independently and under pressure are additional important traits. You will also need self-discipline to start projects on your own, to budget your time, and to meet deadlines and production schedules. Good business sense and sales ability also are important, especially if you plan to freelance or run your own business.

Physical Traits

You will need a good deal of stamina to succeed in this field. For every day that runs smoothly and according to schedule, there will be another that includes deadlines, meetings, rescheduled appointments, problems with suppliers, and just about anything else that can disrupt a carefully planned agenda.

Customers must be interviewed at their convenience. Much of your time will be spent away from your office, often driving to many places and carrying many things. This is especially true for designers who work alone.

You will have to meet with subcontractors and shop for samples and materials. At times you'll work in buildings that are under construction. Travel will be part of your life. In short you will be a very active person. Good health and physical endurance will help you to enjoy the practice of interior design.

Personality Traits

Since working as an interior designer will bring you into regular contact with all sorts of people, from employers to clients to colleagues to suppliers, your personality will play a big part in making your career a success.

First, your attitude toward personal behavior is important. What are your guiding values and principles? Part of this is your attitude toward social conventions and etiquette—in short, your good manners will take you a long way in business.

It's important to remember that interior design is a social profession. As a result, you will most likely meet many different types of people with varying economic, social, educational, and cultural backgrounds. You should be outgoing and express confidence when meeting new people, and you should be willing to accept their differences from you and be open to learn from them. You should also be able to discern their wants and needs and to distill the information you gain into useful information for your projected plans.

Maintaining a positive attitude will also be helpful, because it is the basis for a constructive approach to problems. As mentioned earlier, you are bound to encounter unforeseeable annoyances, such as delays or mistakes in orders, exasperating indecision on the part of customers, or a judgment of your own that you later regret. You'll need cheerfulness and patience to handle all of these situations.

Because you will be dealing with so many different people, a certain amount of disagreement is unavoidable. This is where tact will play a vital role in your business relationships. For example, you must be able to walk the sometimes fine line between carefully pointing out why a client's idea won't work and insulting the client's taste or vision.

Industriousness and dependability are required for any job, and you'll find that these characteristics are linked closely to your creativity as a designer. You will need determination and self-discipline to push yourself to create at your top performance level. This is the drive to put imagination to work.

Since you will often be in a position of having to convince clients of the value of your designs, or to negotiate with suppliers, you'll need the ability to function as a leader. The best way to analyze your leadership ability is to think about the experiences you've had so far. Do friends seek your advice? If you have participated in any school or community organizations, have others listened to your input? Are people interested in your ideas? Your educational program will help you to cultivate your leadership abilities.

Perhaps the most important personality trait you will need in order to become a successful interior designer is moral stamina. This means that you live by two basic ethical principles: honesty and fairness. As an interior designer, you must adhere to the profession's ethical code, in which the basic principles are honesty in conducting your own business and fairness with respect to your dealings with others.

Mental Traits

Whatever your academic abilities may be, it's a very good idea to discipline yourself to think in an analytical and orderly manner. Although initially it might not seem so, these qualities may also be part of the foundation of your creativity. In other words, you must be organized in your thoughts in order to create art.

You will need to be sharp and alert, aware of what is happening around you. You must have strong communication skills, both written and oral. Be sure that you can communicate clearly on paper, by e-mail, and by text message and that you can speak confidently when presenting your ideas. You should also be careful, especially in less-formal communications, such as e-mail and texting, to avoid the pitfall of writing too informally. Remember that your business communications are just that, business, and even a brief note should be grammatically sound and free of slang expressions.

Artistic Talent

You will need artistic talent to be a successful interior designer, as well as a strong degree of intuitive sensitivity to the needs of others.

How do you determine what quantifies your artistic ability? To begin, check these requisites: good eyesight, a steady hand, and adequate training in drafting and rendering. Interior design makes sensitive use of space, shape, color, light, and visual texture. Now add a richness of expression through the use of touch, sound, and smell. Incorporate in your designs the materials you love to touch, sounds you love to hear, and some enticing aromas (such as a cashmere throw, a striking clock, and spicy pine).

And finally, what about your muscular sensibilities? All visual rhythm and balance depend on it. Do you love to play ball? To dance? To ride? Having talents such as these will add to your overall artistic ability.

Are you concerned about the appearance and appeal of your surroundings? Do you respond emotionally as well as intellectually to them? Do you feel the need to create good art through them? It is your need to create in this medium that is the first measure of your artistic ability.

Business Potential

For our purposes, let's separate this necessary ability into two parts. First is your sales ability, which is vital if your prized ideas are to see the light of day. Good selling is the ability to communicate the quality in your design work so that your clients will appreciate it. This type of selling is a necessary part of your professional career.

It's important not to underestimate this commercial aspect of interior design. If you aren't comfortable with it, you might try to enter the interior design field as an assistant or possibly as a teacher. However, if you like to create, to sell your product, and to see it become reality, then you are suited to working as a practicing designer, where you will find rewards in both personal satisfaction and monetary gain.

Selling is only one part of the business picture; you will also need to have shrewd business sense. If you are strictly creative and don't have a business mind, you may want to hire someone to help you with financial management. Although this is an added expense, it will pay for itself if it keeps you from mismanaging the business on your own.

You will get some business training throughout your school training. Pay attention to these classes, especially if you aren't very comfortable or familiar with business matters. Learn what is necessary to make a profit and to keep your business in the black. It's fine if these courses reinforce your feeling that you won't be able to manage the business side of things yourself; at least you'll know before you start your career that you'll need some help in this important area.

4

Preparing for College

Now that you know what the educational requirements are for pursuing a career in interior design, it's time to think about which of the accredited programs is best for you. There are several practical considerations to ponder as you make the important decision about which school to attend.

Selecting a School

There are many factors that can impact the decision of where to go to school. Once you've narrowed down the list of colleges that offer the program you want, you can start to apply other criteria for making the final selection.

For many students economics plays an important part in this selection process. What can you afford? If you dream of attending an out-of-state school but can realistically only afford your state university, you have to think carefully about your priorities and how you will proceed. You may have to make sacrifices to attend the school of your dreams, and you must decide whether they will be worth it. Educational costs and financial aid will be discussed later in this chapter.

There are, of course, other matters besides money to consider. Is the school in a metropolitan area or in a small town? Is it a huge educational complex or a smaller, more intimate campus? You should think about whether you would prefer to be at a smaller, more intimate college or be a more anonymous member of a larger student body.

Although this is a personal decision, some arguments can be made for both sides. If you have never been away from home, a smaller campus may be a smoother transition. It may be easier in this type of setting to make friends and to get to know your professors, who will have a smaller number of students to become acquainted with.

On the other hand, a large campus also has some advantages, especially if it is located in a bigger city. Working opportunities, particularly in interior design, are probably better in an urban area. Design centers will give you firsthand acquaintance with supply sources, and you will see outstanding examples of design. It will be possible for you to observe various aspects of the work, which may help you decide which ones interest you most.

Another plus for the metropolitan setting is its proximity to museums and centers for the performing arts. As an aspiring interior designer with artistic abilities, you will most likely also be interested in cultural activities that enhance your design talents.

Some academic programs include a term of foreign travel or a semester abroad as part of the curriculum. If this is an important factor to you, be sure to research the options at the schools you are considering. This type of opportunity can be invaluable in broadening your horizons both personally and professionally.

Be sure to check the reputations and academic ratings of the schools you are considering. Visit websites, request catalogs, and study course descriptions. You may compare schools at a site such as www.petersons.com, where you can research the pertinent information you'll need to make an informed decision.

One of the best tools in your college search is the campus visit. If possible, visit the campus of any school you plan to apply to in order to gain a real feeling for the atmosphere. Talk to former and present students to get some honest opinions. What is the social life like? How are the student accommodations? Are the off-campus options suitable to your lifestyle?

Once you've selected the school you hope to attend, you have to do what you can to be sure that the school chooses you. The admissions process is an important step, and you should do your best to meet all the requirements. College admission has become very competitive in the last several years, as the number of seventeen- and eighteen-year-olds has greatly increased. In many cases schools have not increased the size of their incoming classes in response to this growth, meaning that there are more applicants than available slots. However, you will most likely find less competition in community colleges and other two-year schools.

Your guidance counselor or senior advisor can be a great resource in guiding you through the application process. If possible, you might want to ask someone you know who has recently completed an application, perhaps a relative or family friend.

Basically, you will have to provide your high school transcript and your score on the Scholastic Aptitude Test (SAT) or on the

ACT, depending on the school's requirements. You will also be asked to document all of your extracurricular activities. If you are still in high school, it's important to participate in clubs, sports, and community events. Be sure to include any volunteer work as well. These activities will show prospective colleges that you understand the importance of social commitment and working as part of a team.

The part of the process that many students worry about is writing the application essay. This is usually a five-hundred-word statement that you will write about yourself. It is an opportunity to relate something about yourself that may not be seen in grades and test scores. Most advisors recommend making a list of possible topics that reflect something about you. For example, you might write about a job you've held, a place where you've spent a lot of time, a hobby you enjoy, a person who is important to you—whatever you choose, your essay should show your passion about the topic and how it has been important in your life. You should write several drafts of the essay until you are comfortable with it.

You will also be asked to provide references. Most schools ask for three letters of recommendation, usually from teachers who can comment on your academic ability and learning potential. It is best to ask teachers from your junior or senior years, if possible in subjects that are related to your intended major.

Be sure to file your college applications by the required deadlines. You should certainly apply to more than one school. Given the competitive nature of college admissions, even the best qualified students are not always accepted by their first choice. Today students are applying to more schools than ever. Some surveys indicate that students apply to as many as seven schools. While you may not find that many schools attractive, there should be three or four that appeal to you.

If you aren't accepted by any of the schools you apply to, don't give up. Take another look at your applications, and be sure that you've met all the admission requirements. Try other schools. You might even consider starting your training at a community college and then transferring to a four-year school later.

Educational Costs

As mentioned earlier, money is an important factor in choosing a school. You must be prepared not only for all your education-related costs, but all your personal costs as well.

School-Related Costs

College tuition can be staggering, especially those at at private universities. In most cases your state university is the least-expensive option for a four-year school. But keep in mind that if you are planning to attend a different state's school, you will most likely pay a higher tuition than in-state residents. You will also probably be considered for acceptance only after resident applicants have all been considered.

Municipal community colleges usually offer the lowest tuition. Many students begin their studies at community colleges and then transfer to a four-year college or university. If your community college counselor knows this is your plan, he or she can help you to choose courses that are most likely to be accepted for transfer credit. It is best in this situation to pursue a basic liberal arts curriculum at the community college and wait until you've transferred to take specialized courses. Tuition in two-year specialty schools, most of which are privately owned and financed, is generally higher than in community colleges.

In any setting, you will also have to pay for books and supplies. If you live on campus, there will be fees for lodging and meals. Commuters will have to pay for transportation or a parking permit.

Personal Expenses

You will also have personal expenses, whether you stay at home or go away to school. Most students have limited funds to spend on personal expenses, so you will probably need to establish a budget in order to make your money last.

If you live in a dorm, you'll want your room to be comfortable and attractive and to reflect a bit of your personality. You can decorate inexpensively, perhaps bringing some things from home. One thing you are sure to keep in your room is electronic equipment. Your computer, MP3 player, cell phone, PDA, television—make sure to clearly label all of these so that you can always identify them.

You'll be working hard and will need time to relax and enjoy yourself. Budget some money for fun, whether it's an occasional movie or concert or a trip to the bookstore or coffee shop. You won't need many special items of clothing, but you should have at least one informal business outfit that may be worn to any occasion that casual clothes won't do. As a design student, you've probably got your own sense of style that you will bring with you to campus and continue to develop as you broaden your education and experience.

Financial Aid

There is no denying that tuition costs are very high, but several forms of financial assistance are available to help ease the burden on students and their families. Aid may be in the form of scholarships, loans, grants, or employment opportunities.

School-administered scholarships are usually limited, although some special scholarships are available through religious and fraternal organizations, labor unions, ethnic societies, and civic groups. If you are interested in this type of assistance, contact any organizations to which you or your parents belong; some might offer financial benefits to members or their children.

Student loans are one of the more common ways of paying for an education. A loan must be repaid, usually beginning after graduation. Loans are provided by private lenders and the federal government, and they are available for both students and parents.

Grants, which do not require repayment, are sometimes awarded to students with exceptional financial need or to those who give promise of exceptional academic excellence. Some of these grants are negotiated through the government. Complete information about the different types of loans and grants is available online. Helpful websites include www.salliemae.com, www.estudentloan.com, www.internationalstudentloan.com/canadian_student, and www.hrsdc.gc.ca/en/learning/canada_student_loan.

Most colleges and universities offer some part-time employment opportunities for qualified students. These jobs are often limited in number and highly sought after by students, so you should inquire as soon as possible about this option.

Start your financial aid requests early, to be sure that you have funds available when it's time to make a tuition payment. Explore as many options as possible to gain the assistance that you need.

Student Organizations

Once you are settled at school, you'll want to join your student chapter of the American Society of Interior Designers (ASID). This will be an important link between your school life and your professional life. Participation in a student chapter provides a social outlet as well as a good professional first step.

Benefits of student membership include:

- *ASID ICON*, a quarterly magazine on cutting-edge design research, business trends, and society news
- *ACCESS*, a student-written newsletter published three times a year
- National scholarship competitions sponsored by the ASID Foundation
- Chapter events, seminars, workshops, continuing education, and competitions, which provide the opportunity to interact with professional designers
- Career days, when ASID professional chapters provide an introduction to the many career options open to interior design students
- Membership card, which can be used for design center admission, some design competitions, chapter program discounts, and more

You will find complete information about student membership and the locations of student chapters at it's website at www.asid.org/studentcenter.

The International Interior Design Association (IIDA) welcomes student members from Canada and the United States. Membership benefits include an annual student mentoring week; a student design competition; and *Custom*, a student newsletter. Visit www.iida.org for information about becoming a student member.

5

Starting Your Career

Once you are ready to apply for a job, where do you start? You may begin right at your school's placement office, where you should be able to find information about careers and further educational opportunities. The placement counselor will want to personally interview you. Tips on how to interview successfully will follow later in this chapter.

You can use the Internet to find a list of interior designers in the area where you wish to work. Search also directories of interior designers or online phone books. If you plan to move to a different city to start your career, be sure that you have enough money saved to get started in a new location and to carry you over until you begin receiving your salary.

Perhaps you will not even need to apply for your first job. If you have made an impression while working at a firm as a student assistant or intern, you may be offered the opportunity to stay on as a junior designer.

Experience Requirement

Experience seems to be a requirement in every field. But how can you give a record of experience if this is your first attempt to get a job in interior design?

From an employer's point of view, the desire for experience is understandable. Although a good apprentice, assistant, aide, or technician can be a benefit, a poor one can be a liability. An employee who misfiles documents and materials, who seems always to be absent at critical times, or who asks frequent unnecessary questions may not be trusted to perform important tasks well. So, it is understandable that a prospective employer is anxious to know about your previous work record.

Some academic programs include a practical learning experience that will give you something to offer when asked about your experience. If you are unable to find a full-time position with an interior design firm, look for other types of employment that can help you to acquire the necessary experience. You should be able to find part-time or temporary work. Most design firms have such positions available for students with good skills in drafting, model making, computer-aided design (CAD), color expertise, furnishing interests, and sales.

There are many opportunities you might consider. Some beginning designers work in showrooms of firms dealing in fine furnishings. Others work in department stores. Both locations provide good initial experience, helping you to learn about carpets, window treatments, wall coverings, furniture and accessories, and in some situations, about antiques. You'll also learn a bit about selling and customer relations.

You might first work with paint and wallpaper companies, furniture manufacturers, lumber outlets, real estate companies, building contractors, office supply houses, and even credit departments. Any of these may provide you with good experience.

Any volunteer work you've done is also important. Think carefully about how any tutoring, child care, or charitable work can be described in terms of what you've learned. Did tutoring advance your communication and leadership skills? Did volunteering at a nursing home teach you to understand the needs of people very different from yourself? Similarly, playing sports may have contributed to your ability to work as part of a team.

Many designers have said that they wished students had more experience with interior design trades. If these are not included in your school's curriculum, try to work for a time in a slipcover and drapery workshop or in one that refinishes or upholsters furniture. Woodworking, wall finishing, carpet installation—knowledge in any of these techniques will help you in your later work.

You should start to think seriously about applying for a job during your last year of school. Begin to assemble your portfolio, which will show the best work you've done in your academic years. In most cases, compiling a portfolio will be a requirement during your senior year.

Résumé and Cover Letter

Your résumé will generally be your introduction to a prospective employer, so it's important to ensure that it makes the best possible first impression. It should concisely present your education and experience, and it should be revised whenever you have pertinent information to add or update.

Because your résumé is so important, it is a good idea to consult one of the many books available that can help you to prepare one.

There are different formats to choose from, and a guide will help you to select the one that is best suited to your situation. You can also find résumé guidance online at sites such as Monster.com and CareerBuilder.com.

It is best to keep your résumé to a single page and to include the following information:

- **Introductory information.** Give your name, address, phone number, and e-mail address but do not include any personal information such as age, marital status, race, religion, and so forth.
- **Type of position sought.** Describe what you are looking for in terms of job requirements, skills, and personal characteristics.
- **Education.** Provide the name and location of your college, date of graduation or number of years attended, and your major. Be prepared to provide a transcript if one is requested, but don't include it with your résumé.

Provide the name and location of your high school, dates of attendance, and major courses taken.

- **Experience.** Include all employers, positions, dates of employment, and responsibilities. List jobs in reverse chronological order, that is, starting with the most recent.
- **Social and professional organizations and experiences.** You can put any affiliations or extracurricular activities in this section.
- **References.** Your résumé should end with "References available upon request."

Be prepared to provide at least three letters of reference if asked; they might be from former employers, teachers, coaches, or a clergy member.

Your résumé should be accompanied by a cover letter. This will explain why you are sending the résumé, and also gives you the opportunity to emphasize in greater detail the aspects of your experience and personality that most strongly correlate to the specific position you are seeking.

If you are responding to a print or online job advertisement, address your letter to the person whose name is listed in the ad. If you are sending the résumé unsolicited, try to address the letter to the person in charge of employment. You might be able to find this information on a company's website, or you may call the human resources department and ask for the information. When responding to an ad, be sure to apply in the manner specified. For example, you may be asked to send your résumé electronically or by fax.

Your letter should convey its message in logical order. Begin by stating your purpose for writing: "I would like to apply for a position as . . ." or "I am responding to your advertisement in the *Kansas City Star* for an interior design assistant." Give any specific information that will clarify the statement, such as "I understand that your design assistant has just resigned," or "When you were on our campus, you suggested that we write to you when our graduation date drew near."

Follow this with a statement about what you think your contribution to the firm may be: "I have had extensive training in CAD and believe my skills would be an asset to Acme Design," or "I have had considerable experience with boating, and I believe I could be valuable to the firm's contract division, which handles transportation designing." If possible, quantify your experience; "ninety hours of carpentry training" sounds more specific and impressive than "much experience in carpentry."

Mention your enclosed résumé. You should avoid repeating the facts that appear there, but it is fine to call attention to important items that you believe would be to your particular advantage: "You will note that I have worked during the summers for XYZ Department Store. During that time, I was promoted from sales clerk to assistant manager of carpet sales." Be as specific as you can about your accomplishments.

Having stated your qualifications, it is appropriate to request an interview. If the company is local, state that you will be available at the interviewer's convenience. If you are applying for a job in a different city, you might mention that you will be there during a specific time period. However, it should be left to the prospective employer to make the final decision about when and where to meet. Conclude with a restatement of your purpose in a slightly different but clear, concise way.

Interview

Sooner or later an employment interview is necessary. The thought of this may make you nervous, but there is really no cause for anxiety. Most firms are eager to learn of fresh new talent, even if they are unable to hire more employees at the time. Many advisors say that the interview is a good experience even if it does not result in a job offer—practice will help you to gain poise and confidence.

During the Interview

You should approach an interview with an attitude of assurance; be as calm, poised, and hopeful as possible. Don't take a negative point of view or advertise your weak points. Don't mention that you are nervous; the interviewer probably knows this and will try to put you at ease. Be certain to be on time for your interview; allow enough time for any possible delays in transportation.

Don't be surprised if the interviewer asks you a number of questions that seem unrelated to the position or your abilities—perhaps about which books you have read recently, what plans you have for your future, what kind of music you prefer. You are being tested on some of the intangibles of your personality—qualities that help an employer gather a larger impression of you than simply your experience and education.

During the interview you will want to learn some things about the work. If the information is not volunteered, be sure to ask. You have a right to know about the organization and what you can expect from it. Like the interviewer, you, too, are interested in intangibles. However, don't ask about such details as medical benefits or vacation time; these are best reserved for a second meeting. Confine your questions to the job itself.

You may be asked about your specific knowledge of aspects of interior design. You may even be asked to answer some questions to test your competency or to do some drawing of a design nature, although your portfolio will usually substitute for this. It will include samples of your work, preferably shown in eight-by-ten glossy photographs.

After the Interview

Try to be aware of cues from the interview that the meeting is drawing to a close. Although it is not desirable to say too little, you also shouldn't talk too much. As one applicant once said, "I suddenly realized that I had the job in the bag if I would just keep quiet."

When you leave, express your appreciation to the interviewer and your wish for a favorable outcome. It might be suitable to ask whether you should make any further inquiry about the position.

If you have convinced the potential employer about your ability to handle the work and your suitability for the job, you have made a positive professional impression, regardless of the outcome. One interviewer was so favorably impressed by a candidate that, although there was no opening at his firm, he took the trouble to recommend the applicant elsewhere.

After an interview, a simple thank-you note is in order. This shows the prospective employer a bit of your public relations skills and reinforces your interest in the position.

Professionalism

Once you accept a position with a design firm, you are a member of the team, and your professional loyalties belong there. Never say anything unfavorable about your employer to outsiders; don't discuss its clients, materials, or methods, except in a positive way. This is simply good business decorum, and it is also in keeping with the ethical code of the American Society of Interior Designers.

You should also never speak disparagingly of a competitor or consciously try to influence one of your rival's clients in your favor. Try to be as helpful as possible at work and maintain a positive attitude, even when things aren't perfect.

Advancement

As a new hire, your first position will probably be as an assistant to a professional interior designer. If all goes well, this experience should quickly lead to complete responsibility for professional undertakings. Try to look ahead and learn beyond your regular job duties. Keep abreast of the markets, and do some independent research and studying to learn of new developments in your field.

It is a good idea to make connections in social, community, and civic areas. This will allow you to meet people who can become part of your professional network and who may lead to new clients or other employment opportunities.

Leaving a Position

When you accept a job, you should be willing to remain with the firm for an adequate period of time to repay it for what seems commensurate with the training you receive. However, there will very likely come a time when, for any of a number of reasons, you will want to make a change. If you are leaving a job on good terms for another position, it is professional to give your employer adequate notice. At least two weeks is expected, four is even better. This may allow you to help train your replacement, if necessary.

Whatever the reason for your departure, you should say as little about it as possible. Don't say anything negative about the job you are leaving or boast about the new one you will be taking. In short don't burn any bridges behind you, since you never know where you may encounter former associates in the future.

Employment Prospects

Employment of interior designers is expected to grow as much as 19 percent through 2016, which is faster than the average for all occupations. Recent increases in homeowner wealth and the growing popularity of home improvement programs on television have increased demand for residential design services. Homeowners have been using the equity in their homes to finance new additions, remodel aging kitchens and bathrooms, and update the general decor of the home. Many homeowners also have requested design help in creating year-round outdoor living spaces. However, this same growth in home improvement television programs and discount furniture stores has spurred a trend in do-it-yourself design, which could hamper employment growth for designers.

As the economy grows, more private businesses and consumers will request the services of interior designers. However, design services are considered a luxury expense and may be subject to fluctuations in the economy. For example decreases in consumer and business income and spending caused by a slow economy may have a detrimental effect on employment of interior designers.

Demand from businesses in the hospitality industry, such as hotels, resorts, and restaurants, should be high because of an expected increase in tourism. The health care industry is also expected to increase opportunities for interior design services because of an anticipated increase in demand for facilities that will accommodate the aging population. Designers will be needed to make these facilities as comfortable and homelike as possible for patients.

Some interior designers choose to specialize in one design element to create a niche for themselves in an increasingly competitive market. The demand for kitchen and bath design is growing in response to the growing demand for home remodeling. Designs using the latest technology in, for example, home theaters, state-of-the-art conference facilities, and security systems are expected to be especially popular. In addition, demand for home spas, indoor gardens, and outdoor living spaces should continue to increase.

Extensive knowledge of ergonomics and green design are also expected to be in demand. Ergonomic design has gained in popularity with the growth in the elderly population and workplace safety requirements. The public's growing awareness of environmental quality and the growing number of individuals with allergies and asthma are expected to increase the demand for green design and construction.

Interior designers are expected to face keen competition for available positions because many talented individuals are attracted to this profession. Individuals with little or no formal training in interior design, as well as those lacking creativity and perseverance, will find it very difficult to establish and maintain a career in this occupation.

6

Custom and
Contract Designing

As you establish your career, you will have to decide whether you prefer to work in custom or contract design. In custom design, you will deal with individual clients, as opposed to contract work, which serves larger clients and is generally considered bigger business.

A Studio of Your Own

Working in custom design or private practice usually means that you are dealing with smaller, private clients. It often carries the suggestion of exclusiveness and high cost, since custom clients were once exclusively wealthy. Today the phrase frequently means that the created interiors are planned for the satisfaction of one person or a small group and that the client desires a personalized solution. This can still mean a high-end budget as well as a more moderate cost.

Specifically we are talking about interior designing by a small studio for the needs of clients who want a one-of-a-kind design for a home or some not-too-large enterprise, such as a clubhouse, a small restaurant, a library, or a store.

A custom studio may be organized as a private ownership, a partnership, or a small corporation. The greater the number of business participants, the less the individual financial risk—however, this may also decrease the possibility of individual taste, standards, and choice of clients.

Although private practice may be one of the most rewarding ways of working as an interior designer, it is generally not for those who are new to the field. It is better to gain experience in both design and business practices working for an established designer before you open your own private studio.

To set up your own design studio, you'll need some knowledge of law and finance. You probably will have learned some of this in school, but it is a good idea to consult an attorney and an accountant who are qualified in the area of opening a business.

If you enter into a partnership, be sure that you know your colleagues and their skills and integrity before sharing your career with them. It is also important to make a partnership legal, which will protect you and all other parties equally.

Getting Started

Whichever business structure you choose, you will need operating capital. How much? In round figures, about enough to run the establishment from four to six months or until the firm has been able to turn over an inventory and operate profitably.

Where does the money come from? Many entrepreneurs use their savings, money borrowed from or invested by family and friends, or bank loans. A corporation may raise funds by issuing stock.

Both your customers and your business should pay promptly—the one guarantees interest, the other discounts. Paying your suppliers in installments or making late payments can be costly. You will pay interest in both situations, and paying up front will often result in a discount.

How will you be spending this capital? First you'll need a place of business. Even if you work from home, remember that you'll need at least one room used exclusively for your business. You can also look for office space to rent. The cost of this is charted against business, so if you use space in your home, you may take it as a deduction on your income tax.

You'll need to spend a bit of money to outfit your office, but with some careful shopping, you should be able to keep the cost down. Decorating your space need not be too expensive, if you use your creative talents to make it interesting and expressive of your taste. If clients will be visiting your office, you'll want it to make a positive impression. Even without visitors, an attractive work space will help you to produce better designs.

You will need to purchase an initial inventory of samples and furnishing catalogs. Try to limit your selection by planning to deal with as few firms as possible to carry out the type of work you plan to do. In many cities, you can take a client to a design center or showroom to see firsthand what you have in mind.

One of the areas in which you can save money is buying office equipment. You should be able to find used furniture that is attractive and reasonably priced. You'll need a computer, of course. It might be a good idea to invest in a laptop so that you can bring it along on projects. To round out your office equipment, you should have a printer and copy machine. An economical choice is a multifunctional unit that serves as a printer, scanner, copy machine, and answering machine.

You will also need a dedicated phone and fax line. You might decide to use a voice-mail system for messages so that you can access it remotely and not miss any important calls.

You should also establish a strong website, which can be a powerful marketing tool. If you have the ability to set up a site yourself, by all means do so, but there are many services available that can help you to do this without spending too much money. A website will help cut down on the amount of inventory you need to keep, and it will show prospective clients some examples of jobs you've completed.

There are other business expenses. An accounting system is important for keeping accurate records. Many small business owners use Quickbooks software, which is tailored to specific industries. The system allows you to back up your data to give to your accountant for tax preparation. You will also have to decide whether you need an administrative assistant to manage business details.

You are entitled to some small wage even at the very early stage of your business. Unfortunately, as the owner, your personal salary is paid last. The profit on the capital must come first, which means that you may have to exist on your savings for a time.

You will need to keep some money accessible. A basic rule of thumb is to keep on hand enough cash to pay for installments on large purchases of goods and equipment.

Making the Business Work

Keeping your business solvent will require hard work, attention to management, and favorable economic conditions. Your company is a hard-won reality, and it is up to you to keep expenses to a minimum and maximize your income in order to accomplish your goals.

To be successful, you will need a sufficient number of clients to justify your capital expenditure, and you will have to keep those clients satisfied. You'll accomplish this by selling a good product—this is where your designing skill and your personality enter the picture.

Not every designer has all of the abilities needed to run a studio. So before you decide to open your own business, appraise yourself honestly and either take in a partner who can supplement your talents with business acumen or join a firm where you will not be responsible for business decisions.

Contract Designing

Contract designing involves providing designs under contract for big business clients. A contract is a legal agreement between producer and receiver. It implies that a specific agreement with respect to the nature of the work and the manner of fulfilling the assignment is legally bound in contract form. Firms that work with the public on these terms are considered to be contract firms.

Contract firms usually handle large jobs with big budgets. The work often involves the use of identical specified products, as when a hospital assignment requires many beds; however, a contract order might also require some custom-made, one-of-a-kind articles. An interior designer working with such a firm is known as a contract interior designer.

This type of work is generally highly specialized. A contract firm might use the services of a score of drafters or computer experts (CAD designers). It might employ designers who specialize in planning the interiors of churches, schools, hospitals, retirement homes, and other types of specialty buildings. It might use space planners; specialists in lighting, color, equipment, plumbing, heating, and safety; spec writers; and schedule managers. All these workers are skilled in some phase of interior design, and they come together in a multifaceted process that requires cooperation in order to meet the client's needs.

Contract Clients

Who does a contract firm work for? Often it is another large corporation—a hospital, hotel, restaurant, office, merchandising establishment, or even the government. Both designer and client are part of the big industrial-business complex that characterizes today's business world. Given this fact, no other method of handling the design needs of these clients would work as well as the contract method, in light of its structure for maintaining the order of an assignment.

Suppliers

The contract branch of interior design is supported by a gigantic army of specialized trades and industries, some of which employ their own designers. Designers need to purchase wall coverings, window treatments, carpets, art, furniture, lighting—just about anything that you can imagine in a building interior.

Since contract design is a business, design firms also need to purchase their own business supplies—everything from pens to computers to janitorial supplies. Large companies have purchasing departments that establish relationships with suppliers. If you work in a contract design firm, you will have to follow company procedure for ordering supplies for your projects.

Financial Aspect of Contract Designing

Contract designing has evolved in response to a need. The increasing number of schools, hospitals, resorts, cruise ships, and other specialty buildings should ensure the continuing need for this type of firm.

In light of this, we should consider the difference between those areas of interior design that are devoted to private and generally smaller production and those that work on large contracts.

One principal difference is in the financial system each area employs. The custom designer may be paid by a fee, a commission, a percentage of the total order, or a salary. The contract firm, as its name implies, operates on a contract basis, receiving a percentage of the total bill. However, contract firms may also deal on a consultation fee basis for services performed. As long as the terms are clear and agreed upon by both parties, it does not much matter which method is employed.

If contract work is paid for as a percentage of the total commodity bill, the percentage per item is of course much lower than it would be in custom work. There is a difference between the amount of time required in specifying one hundred duplicate chairs and the amount of time needed to detail one hundred separate ones. This difference results in a higher markup per individual article in custom assignments.

Advantages and Disadvantages of Contract Work

As a new designer entering the field, what is the advantage of entering contract work rather than private practice? In the first place, jobs may be more readily available. If you have some particular skills and feel more suited to specialized work, you may find more opportunities to use those talents in a contract design firm.

But there can also be some disadvantages in contract designing. You are never more than part of a finished product, even though you may have worked as part of a team from beginning to end. There is not quite the sense of involvement or the satisfaction of an individually conceived and executed project, nor is there the same amount of publicity attained from a successful one. This situation, of course, will vary with the size of the firm and with its particular policies.

Again, contract work is probably more lucrative than an individual practice, particularly when you are just starting out, and it offers opportunities for broadening your range of experience as you observe large design projects.

How the Work Progresses

As in any design setting, the first step of a project is securing a client. Most design firms avoid blatant advertising, relying instead on successfully completed projects to create an image that interests and attracts customers. Satisfied clients are the best advertisement of all; word-of-mouth recommendations can bring many new projects.

Your client may be considering other firms, so there will have to be preliminary meetings to establish the client's needs. These meetings will be followed by a proposal that suggests solutions with drawn plans and budget estimates. The scope of these preliminary steps will vary depending on the size and expense of the project. This phase of the work is time consuming and may ultimately be unrewarding. That is the risk inherent in this type of work, when a client may decide that another firm better meets its needs.

Legal expertise is an important part of the process in such large projects. Before signing a final agreement, the firm must have guaranteed itself against inflation, against the financial future of its client, and against any chance of the client's wishing to retract or change plans at some future time.

Early in the undertaking, it may be necessary to establish a professional relationship with the architect who is connected with the project in question, if the contract firm is not primarily an architectural one with an interior design department. The architect must be kept informed of the interior design requirements related to architectural, mechanical, electrical, and plumbing systems. The information must be itemized, costs detailed, and cost liabilities assigned. All participants must know exactly what is expected of each contributing firm and from which budget each of the costs will be paid. Time schedules require careful coordination.

From this point the work in a contract design firm progresses much as described in earlier chapters. It is a question of scheduling, spec writing, confirming orders, business accounting, installations, work supervision, inspections, and final payments. In many cases there is also a gala affair to celebrate completion.

In many respects contract work is no different from any project in the design field except that it is larger and by implication involves far more repetitive work and installments. So it is usually financed in a different way, it may allow you to work as a more specialized designer, and it may provide a higher salary.

Your First Job

Your degree from an accredited and respected design program may qualify you for a position in a prestigious contract firm. Your initial job will probably be in a minor capacity, wherever your skills are most needed and useful and where you will also learn a great deal.

Once your abilities are recognized, you will find yourself closer to the real designing. At this point you may be called a junior designer. As you gain more expertise, you may be given an assignment as the designer in charge of a project, which means that you will have the overall responsibility of seeing that the team's concept is carried out. The designing itself will probably not be entirely your work but rather that of the group; as stated earlier, contract work is company work. However, at this point, your name may appear whenever the project gets publicity. Most reputable firms are generous about giving credit because the firm's name appears along with the designer's.

In the course of time you may become the senior designer. Then you not only will have your name affixed to a design project but also will place your stamp on all projects that you work on.

7

RELATED FIELDS

YOUR TRAINING IN interior design will qualify you for many career opportunities within the field. You may also find an interest in a related area. In this chapter we will look at some of the possibilities.

Interior Design Specializations

Even if you choose an area of specialization, it's still a good idea to keep an open mind about the others, since a broader knowledge base can only widen your potential for the future.

You may even complete your educational program and then find that your interests lie along the line of some specialty, such as lighting, color, or space planning. Specializing might also focus on specific and current social interests such as energy control, sound control, or safety conditioning. One of these might become your specialty to use in a designing firm or later in your own studio.

Study and research your chosen specialty, and gain some degree of experience that can help to advance your career. Remember that each new job will be a learning experience, and if done well, an indirect advertisement of your talents. In time, your specialty may well become your major activity.

Related Fields

Your education and personal interests may take you in a different direction. Following is an alphabetical listing of some of the many positions that are indirectly related to your interior design training that may appeal to you.

Antiques

You may find that the historical knowledge you have acquired leads you to an interest in antiques. This might include acquiring and selling antiques, preparing appraisals, restoring antiques, or writing about them.

It has often been said that dealing in antiques is not a business, it's a mania, and those who are afflicted know how to find a position in the field. But even if this is so, you must know the goods and the class of furnishings you will be dealing with.

Depending on your credentials, you may look for work with a reputable or nationally known dealer. Consult the publication *The Magazine Antiques* (www.themagazineantiques.com), which publishes information about collecting, museums, auctions, and other resources for professionals in antiques. You might also consider submitting an article to the magazine.

In addition to studying the magazine, you should visit museum collections and train your eye to recognize the value of a piece. Develop your selling ability, and learn to help people make decisions that you think are to their advantage as well as your own.

Commission Art

If your artistic ability lies in drawing, painting, sculpture, or a craft, you may choose to work in this arena. Commission art is artwork that you either sell yourself as your own agent or through an independent firm that sells its services. You might become connected with a design firm that uses your art in its projects.

This sort of service demands the highest degree of a specialized talent. Exhibit your work wherever you can; you may find that a unique quality will build your reputation.

Computer Management

You may be able to combine your design talent and computer skills to carve out a niche in the industry. You might work as an entrepreneur, selling your services to individual firms that need someone to design websites, coordinate programs, and offer instruction to staff members. Smaller firms might also hire you to help with computer issues. Your skill as a designer will be a plus in making clients feel confident in your ability to understand their business and offer them the appropriate assistance.

Consultant

You may find consulting work as an interior designer, charging clients a fee for services rendered. You may even find work with other designers, particularly if you have a specialty that is in demand.

You must have a good design reputation to succeed as a consultant. It will also be helpful to have a website, color charts, samples, a photograph library, and access to showrooms. This is usually a job for experienced designers, but if it is your goal, try to find jobs that will give you the expertise you'll need to consult.

Crafts

Craftsworkers are self-motivated, generally by a true love of their art. Perhaps you learned a skill in your training, such as weaving, woodworking, metalworking, ceramics, or painting. Or you may have a natural talent that you've practiced and expanded on in your studies. If you hope to have a career in crafts, you'll need to test your abilities in local exhibits.

Designer with Building Development Firms

Most developers of residential subdivisions and condominiums offer model units that potential buyers may visit to see the interior of the home. In many cases, several models are available to show the differences among the various styles. For example, a subdivision might include models of two-, three-, and four-bedroom homes.

Each of these units is tastefully decorated to give the public an idea of what the finished home may look like. Some developers operate on a national level, and working for them may involve traveling to different sites around the country.

The chance to design model homes may not always be readily available. However you can inquire with your local contracting companies. Most large developers advertise in the real estate sections of major newspapers. Another possibility is to apply for an office position in this type of firm and learn about the company that way. Once you've become established with the company, you might suggest your design abilities to your superiors.

Display and Exhibition Positions

This kind of work is similar to stage designing although with less focus on historical accuracy. Creating displays for stores is only one aspect of the work. Display artists are also employed by industrial companies for traveling exhibitions, where they arrange changing presentations for merchandise marts and showrooms. Even museums use designers for planning the backgrounds for their exhibits.

Learn who heads the display work at your local stores. There might also be a community group that needs design volunteers to help promote its image. After all, displays are forms of advertising. If you have the inclination, cultivate the talent.

Equipment Specialist

Many firms, such as dealers in kitchen supplies or other furnishing equipment, employ a specialist to position their wares for the best possible presentation to customers. Familiarity with the items on display will be a help; you might visit showrooms, high-end furniture stores, and home expo centers to get a feel for this type of work.

Fashion Forecaster

As someone interested in design, you have read articles about trends and new styles. Who writes these articles? Generally it is an interior designer whose solid historical background in the field has contributed to a sense of how to forecast the future.

If you have strong writing skills, you might try combining them with your knowledge of interior design to produce articles. Submit them to your local newspaper, or research online publications and other magazines that might be interested in purchasing your work.

Government Work

The government also offers opportunities for interior designers. For example offices, embassies, historic sites, museums, and any number of other government sites require the work of designers. At the time of this writing, there are openings for interior designers at a Department of Veterans Affairs hospital and for an exhibit specialist with the Smithsonian Institute.

A good deal of government design work is contracted by private industry. The American Society of Interior Designers regularly works with federal government agencies, including the Department of Housing and Urban Development, the Small Business Administration, and the Consumer Product Safety Commission.

To look for jobs offered directly by the government, visit www.usajobs.com. For federal design jobs in Canada, visit www.jobs-emplois.gc.ca.

Historic Preservation and Restoration

This is a growing area that may provide opportunities for interior designers who specialize in the history of buildings and furnishings. This knowledge extends to restoration procedures.

Adaptive reuse is an important phase of this work, in which old buildings are adapted to today's purposes while still preserving the spirit of their own age. If you are able to interpret the spirit of the past and express it through design, this field may interest you.

Jobs in this area may be with local agencies that are engaged in actual restoration of historical home sites and libraries. You might help your job search by getting involved with a local group interested in historic buildings.

Check with your city government to see whether it is planning any historic renovation projects. Civic groups might also be involved in such projects, and architectural firms may also have some leads.

If you are interested in this field, you might be able to find a school that offers a program in historic orientation, particularly at the graduate level.

You may also find information through the National Trust for Historic Preservation, which is an advisory and educational organization devoted to the preservation of the nation's landmarks. Visit www.nthp.org for information about the trust and its work. In Canada visit the Historic Places Initiative at www.pc.gc.ca/progs/plp-hpp.

Museum Work

A good deal of work in museums is concerned with the decorative arts. There are entry-level positions on lecturing, restoration, curatorial, and teaching staffs, all of which may provide valuable experience for a future career. You might aspire to working in exhibit design or to specializing in overall museum work. The best advice is to apply at a local museum and keep learning.

Photography

Some people find that photographing interiors is an even more challenging specialty than interior design itself. It involves knowledge of both professions—your photographs must convey a sense of the space organization, impart the emotional tone, and focus the viewer's attention on the important objects. It is a real skill and art, and it may involve a substantial financial investment for equipment.

Photograph your own or a colleague's designs, and try to have the results published in a local magazine or paper. A lead photograph of an interior by some prominent designer might be done in a way sufficiently outstanding to gain some recognition.

Stage Designing

Your training as an interior designer is good preparation for this work. Most plays need stage sets, and you can make them effective, authentic in style, and perhaps improvise them at the lowest cost.

Look for volunteer work at your local community theater. You may have to devote a great deal of time, labor, and skill in order to receive any reward, but if this is where your interests lie, it can be worthwhile.

Staging for Real Estate

Most real estate agents advise their clients who are selling homes on how to help their houses make the best impression on buyers. They may recommend removing clutter, putting away personal photos, cleaning, and touching up finishes. But what about a brand-new house that is empty or one with furnishings that are so old they make a negative image?

In these cases realtors often recommend staging the house, which basically means redecorating the interior to make it more attractive. This is a good opportunity for both professional interior designers and those who are not licensed, who can either work independently or directly for a real estate firm. If you work as an independent stager, you will need to keep an inventory of furniture, lamps, artwork, and floor coverings. You'll also need a place to store these items.

Store-Home Consultant

Many high-end stores offer consulting services to shoppers; some of these advisory positions do not require the expertise of a professional interior designer. These jobs are usually tied closely with the store's merchandise.

Teaching

You will need at least a master's degree for teaching at the college level, and a Ph.D. may be preferred. Some experience in the field is always a plus, but your solid academic training may suffice if you hope to teach interior design. You may also teach on a part-time basis as an adjunct faculty member at a vocational school or community college. Many of these positions may be in specialized areas of expertise, such as design, rendering, workroom practices, or business disciplines.

You might also look for opportunities with professional organizations such as the American Society of Interior Designers or the Interior Designers of Canada, teaching continuing education courses or leading seminars and workshops.

Television

The popularity of interior design has led to a number of television shows on the subject. Even some local cable stations and public television stations air programs on interior design. If you hope to write or report for one of these shows, you will definitely need experience in the field.

You should know your subject very well and be able to project your enthusiasm for it to others. It is also important to convey confidence through an attractive persona and pleasant speaking voice. If you are interested in this area, it might be a good idea to take some drama and voice classes.

Writing

Like creating your own art, if writing is your passion, you are most likely already drawn to it and may be able to combine your talent with your ability in interior design.

First you need to decide what type of writing you wish to pursue. Would you like to write for a newspaper, magazine, or online publication? Do you aspire to write a book? Whatever you decide, you'll need to do some research. If you plan to write for magazines, find out which are the most appropriate for your work and learn their submission processes. If you want to write a book, you should know which publishers handle the type of book you are planning to write and the proper format for submitting a manuscript.

There are resources available to help you with your research and with your writing. Visit www.writersdigest.com and www.writers market.com for information about approaching agents and editors, formatting a manuscript, and payment rates for publications.

A Final Thought

This list of employment opportunities is by no means all-inclusive. Like so many industries, interior design is a field that continues to evolve while keeping up with such factors as cultural changes and technological advances. You are by nature a creative person, and if you combine your creativity with imagination and solid academic training, you may find yourself designing an entirely new career.

8

PROFESSIONAL ORGANIZATIONS

THERE ARE A number of professional organizations for interior designers. This chapter will give you an overview of several of them, including benefits of membership and contact information.

You should keep in mind that professional organizations also exist for most of the sub-areas of interior design, such as furniture, textiles, and lighting. You may have occasion to contact some of these other associations throughout your career.

In general a professional organization has four major purposes: to improve its collective image, to help young practitioners establish continuity in the profession, to create mutually beneficial relations with similar organizations, and to contribute toward social good. It must uphold an educational standard and must subscribe to a code of ethics in order to fulfill professional goals.

American Society of Interior Designers

This consolidated group of professional interior designers is the largest organization of its kind in the world. It serves more than thirty-eight thousand members through a network of forty-eight chapters throughout the United States and Canada.

The American Society of Interior Designers (ASID) is open to all qualified designers in any specialty, whether they are employed in private practice, contract, institutional, or government work. This makes the organization the one effective body able to advance the needs of all who are professionally practicing under its jurisdiction. Members of the organization may use the initials ASID after their names, indicating to colleagues and clients that they are professionally affiliated.

ASID Group Responsibilities

The first of the organization's group responsibilities is education. ASID sets the educational requirements for its membership and assists American and Canadian schools in maintaining high and relevant standards for the education of interior designers.

In addition to working on all phases of educational improvement, ASID mandates that its members and the schools that carry out its educational purposes are equipped with the latest knowledge of theory or fact bearing on the profession. This means keeping abreast of information on many topics, such as new materials, technology, building codes, government regulations, flammability standards, design psychology, and product performance, among others. The ASID accomplishes this through sponsored academic courses, seminars, group meetings, workshops, and a program of self-teaching exercises.

The second of the ASID professional functions is the establishment of the code of ethics under which it operates. ASID members are required to conduct their professional practice in a manner that will command the respect and confidence of their clients, suppliers, colleagues, and the general public. Every member of the society subscribes to a professional code that upholds the laws and regulations of the group regarding business procedures and the practice of interior design. It clearly states the allowable manner of functioning with respect to compensation, competence in execution, and details of written-contract and client relations.

Categories of Membership

There are seven categories of ASID membership, ensuring that interior designers at every level of expertise are represented by the organization.

1. **Professional.** This highest level of membership is for those who have completed a specified course of accredited education and work experience in interior design and who have passed the National Council for Interior Design Qualification (NCIDQ) examination. Canadian designers who are members of the Association of Registered Interior Designers of Ontario (ARIDO) may transfer this membership to ASID.

2. **Educator (professional).** This level is for educators who are actively employed as full-time instructors or department chairs in a postsecondary program of interior design education. Employment must be at any university or accredited school of interior design that requires completion of forty semester credit hours in interior design–related courses. Applicants must have successfully passed the NCIDQ exam.

3. **Allied.** This level is open to practicing interior designers who have completed forty semester or sixty quarter credit hours in interior design education from an accredited institution (university, college, or technical school). Applicants must provide an official college transcript and/or technical school records; continuing education coursework/hours are not accepted toward meeting the education requirement.

4. **Educator (allied).** Educators who are actively engaged as department chairs or full-time instructors in a postsecondary program of interior design education at any university or accredited school of interior design that requires completion of forty semester credit hours in interior design–related courses are eligible. Application requirements include an official college transcript and/or technical school records verifying receipt of degree, a detailed job description, and a letter verifying employment as an educator.

5. **International.** This is open to qualified interior designers whose residence and principal place of business lie outside the boundaries of an ASID chapter. Applicants must provide an official college transcript and/or technical school records verifying the degree earned.

6. **Student.** Membership is available to students who are currently enrolled in an interior design or interior architecture program that requires at least forty credit hours of design-related course work. Those attending schools with an ASID student chapter may join as a student chapter member; those at other schools may join as an independent student member. ASID student members may advance to allied membership upon graduation.

7. **Industry partner.** Eligible members include interior design industry manufacturers and their representatives, related trade associations, and market centers. This membership level provides many

opportunities for interaction between interior designers and the interior furnishings industry that supplies services and manufactured products.

You can find complete information about the ASID by contacting the society directly:

American Society of Interior Designers
608 Massachusetts Avenue NE
Washington, DC 20002
www.asid.org

Interior Designers of Canada

The Interior Designers of Canada (IDC) is a national association of seven provincial interior design associations. It works to advance the profession and to promote high quality in education and practice nationwide. Designers must be members at the highest level of their provincial association to use the designation IDC with their names.

The provinces that maintain interior design associations are British Columbia, Alberta, Saskatchewan, Manitoba, Ontario, New Brunswick, and Nova Scotia. IDC represents designers in the following four areas.

1. **Education.** IDC supports quality assurance for interior design education programs in Canadian universities and colleges through its affiliation with the Council for Interior Design Accreditation, which establishes the criteria for accreditation of interior design education programs.

2. **Professional qualification.** IDC recognizes the international NCIDQ qualifying exam, which is used throughout Canada and the United States.

3. **Continuing education.** IDC is a partner in the continuing education system used by the profession in Canada and the United States. Continuing education courses are developed by experts and approved by an international committee. Courses cover the complete range of topics in interior design.

4. **Liaisons.** IDC represents the interior design profession to the federal government and various organizations and forums, ensuring that Canadian designers are represented internationally and kept informed on current issues.

You can find additional information about IDC and links to the provisional associations by contacting:

Interior Designers of Canada
226-6 Adelaide Street East
Toronto, ON M5C 1H6
www.interiordesigncanada.org

Interior Design Educators Council

The Interior Design Educators Council (IDEC) studies various aspects of interior design education. Benefits of membership in IDEC include an annual conference featuring speakers, reports, seminars, and exhibits; annual regional conferences in the five IDEC regions; *e-RECORD*, an electronic newsletter; the semiannual refereed *Journal of Interior Design*; juried exhibitions; career guidance; and networking opportunities. Membership is available at several levels:

- **Professional.** This highest level is open to full-time interior design educators in colleges, universities, art schools, community and junior colleges, and trade and technical schools and institutes. Requirements include a diploma, bachelor's degree or master's degree in interior design or a related field from an accredited school; two years of experience as a full-time interior design educator in a department offering a program in interior design; and a passing score on the NCIDQ exam.

- **Associate.** This level is for part-time interior design educators and for those who do not meet the requirements for professional membership. A full-time educator who has completed two years of interior design education experience and meets qualifications for professional membership may transfer from associate to professional status.

- **Graduate.** Students enrolled in a professional postgraduate degree program may apply for graduate membership.

- **Honorary.** This invitational category is designed to recognize significant contributions to interior design education by individuals not eligible to be professional members.

- **Fellow.** This is a professional membership category intended to honor a member who has made an outstanding contribution to the IDEC.

- **Educator affiliate.** Part-time and adjunct interior design educators are eligible for this level.

- **Industry affiliate.** This category is for industry allies interested in interior design education and the activities of IDEC. Its purpose is to strengthen relations and communications between education and practice.

- **Retired.** This is available to members who are officially retired from their educational institution or design-related practice.

• **Inactive.** This category is open to professional members of at least five years who are temporarily not engaged in interior design education.

You may find complete information about IDEC by contacting:

IDEC Headquarters
7150 Winton Drive, Suite 300
Indianapolis, IN 46268
www.idec.org

Council for Interior Design Accreditation

The Council for Interior Design Accreditation (CIDA) is an independent, nonprofit organization that accredits interior design education programs at colleges and universities in the United States and Canada. Accreditation is based on the following criteria: program objectives, educational program, students, faculty, resources and facilities, administration, and community relations.

Nearly two hundred volunteers from interior design practice and education perform the work of CIDA, which currently accredits approximately 150 interior design programs.

The IDEC website provides complete information on interior design and accredited programs. Go to www.idec.org.

International Federation of Interior Architects/Designers

The International Federation of Interior Architects/Designers (IFI), as its name implies, is a federation of the organizations of the individual participating countries. Its current membership represents fifty-two member associations, institutions, and schools in forty-five countries on every continent. The IFI collectively represents over twenty-five thousand individual practicing interior designers worldwide.

Like other professional organizations, the IFI has a code of ethics to which members must adhere. It also holds biannual international conventions, as well as numerous workshops, meetings, and other events at cities throughout member countries.

The IFI has established minimum standards for both interior design education and professional qualification. Education should include: fundamentals of design and basic knowledge of materials; visual communication; environmental concerns; completion of four major creative projects; interpretation of working drawings and building technology; and professional practice.

The IFI has its headquarters in Singapore. For complete information on the association, visit the website at www.ifiworld.org.

National Council for Interior Design Qualification

This nonprofit organization supervises the qualifying examination for interior design professional competence. A passing score on the National Council for Interior Design Qualification examination indicates that an individual has met minimum competency standards for the practice of interior design. Passing the exam is a requirement for licensure in all NCIDQ member jurisdictions. The exam is also a qualification for professional membership in interior design organizations.

NCIDQ sponsors the Interior Design Experience Program (IDEP) for entry-level designers. IDEP assists entry-level interior designers in obtaining a broad range of quality professional experience that is required for taking the NCIDQ exam. It also aids in the transition between formal education and professional practice.

The two-day exam includes two comprehensive multiple-choice sections and a practicum section. The first multiple-choice section, Principles and Practices of Interior Design, consists of 100 scored questions and 25 unscored experimental questions on programming, schematic design, and design development. The second section, Contract Documents and Administration, consists of 125 scored and 25 unscored experimental questions. It covers contract documents, contract administration, and professional practice.

In the practicum section, Schematics and Design Development, candidates are required to produce a design solution that requires preparing schematics, producing plan drawings, and developing appropriate specifications.

For complete information on NDICQ and the exam, contact:

NDICQ
1200 Eighteenth Street NW, Suite 1001
Washington, DC 20036
www.ndicq.org

9

FUTURE OF INTERIOR DESIGN

As YOU READ in Chapter 5, the outlook for a career in interior design is quite good. The very nature of the profession, with changing customs, trends, and tastes, means that there will be room for new ideas and practices. Technological advances and demographic changes will also contribute to new procedures.

In this chapter we will look at some of the current and emerging issues that should impact the future of interior design.

Large Enterprises

Mergers and consolidations have become a staple of the business world, often creating huge new enterprises that require massive headquarters. This ensures much new building or, at the very least, renovating and furnishing.

This development has certainly had an impact on the interior design profession, and this will most likely continue. For one thing it creates a need for more large design firms to accommodate the increasing number of large contract clients. Specialists in every phase of interior design may find work in these firms. Many large companies that handle the entire task of building and furnishing employ architects, landscape architects, interior designers, and craftsworkers. Some of these operate primarily as architecture firms, others as interior design firms. In either case, they operate with the professional groups working independently, similar to the way a number of medical specialists might work in a group practice, calling on one another's services as needed.

Technological Advances

Technology has led to many advances in interior design. Designers may use computers to analyze client needs, coordinate projects, and retrieve information. However, the biggest impact of technology on interior design is computer-aided design, or CAD.

Using CAD systems, designers are required to do far less drafting and rendering. The precision and speed with which designs may be planned is a valuable tool. A CAD program may incorporate two- and three-dimensional drawings, as well as special topics, such as isometric drawings and presentations that include layouts, a sheet set, and a Web page.

Your academic training will include instruction in CAD. In addition to general knowledge, you may also learn to use the technology in specialized areas, such as kitchen or bath design, retail design, or lighting design.

Computer-activated films have also helped educators to teach fundamental space concepts. The ability to see tangible changes can help students to visualize conceptual relationships that are difficult to demonstrate.

A Global Market

Many business relationships cross borderlines. American and Canadian firms have markets and offices in Europe, the Mideast, the Far East, and South America; foreign countries have outlets in North America. This global market presents many opportunities for young designers with language skills.

Design Exchange

Many American interior design ideas are implemented abroad. American influence is seen in motel chains with tastefully and functionally designed rooms. Shopping malls are built with emphasis on coordinated interior design, on considering space planning so as to route traffic, and on a certain dramatic quality of fun that makes shopping a form of entertainment. These are just a few ideas that make American interior design profitable in other countries.

This is, of course, a reciprocal relationship. Many projects in the United States and Canada incorporate foreign design elements. Asian-styled decorations, Oriental carpets, Tudor construction, and Scandinavian furnishings are just a few of the international styles that are used in North American design.

Education Exchange

Interior designers who are interested in this global sharing of styles understand the importance of the exchange of instruction in schools, which may involve faculty exchange and visits, cultural exchange of course content, and student exchange.

Many schools in North America have introduced studies that involve the interchange of ideas between students of different cultures. This may include short visits from foreign instructors or North American teachers making brief trips abroad. These studies offer the opportunity for extensive research, which inevitably leads to better cultural understanding.

Many academic programs also provide the opportunity for students to study abroad. Some of these trips are short-term, perhaps involving a group that travels together for a summer session. Others might last for an entire semester. The obvious benefits of international study are increased multicultural awareness and improved language skills, not to mention an overall sense of maturity that you might gain from interacting with a wider variety of designers.

Growing Trends

There are several current trends that are likely to have a strong impact on the field of interior design. We will briefly examine some of these trends and their potential influence on interior design.

Aging in Place

As the baby boomer generation ages, we are experiencing unprecedented growth in the number of people age sixty-five and older. With awareness of better nutrition, healthier lifestyles, and advances in medicine, this growth rate is expected to continue well into the twenty-first century.

Studies indicate that as many as eight in ten homeowners age forty-five and older want to stay in their homes as long as possible, even if they may need help caring for themselves in order to do so. In addition more people are welcoming elderly parents into their households. Most homes will require some renovations to ensure the safety and happiness of aging residents.

This desire to remain in one's home for as long as possible—called *aging in place*—offers a great many opportunities for residential interior designers. Whether a client plans to build a new home or remodel an older one, interior design services may be very valuable in planning for future needs.

The changes that might be made to accommodate older residents include installing grab bars in showers and tubs, brighter lighting, and nonskid floor surfaces. Larger renovations may include moving the master bedroom and laundry area to the main floor or installing a walk-in shower with a seat.

The National Association of Home Builders offers the Certified Aging-in-Place Specialist Program, which provides comprehensive information about working with older adults to remodel their homes. Many interior designers elect to pursue this certification. Visit www.nahb.org for information about the certification process.

The American Society of Interior Designers (ASID) offers detailed information about aging-in-place designing. For more information, relevant articles, and links to other helpful sites, visit www.asid.org.

Universal Design

Maturing and elderly residents are not the only people who may need to make changes in their homes in order to maintain their long-term safety and security. People with disabilities or certain physical ailments may also benefit from interior changes that help them to function in their homes.

Rather than finding solutions to individual situations, there is a movement toward universal design, in which all homes would be designed to accommodate all ages and physical needs. With universal design, people with very different needs can all enjoy the same home. This concept also helps to eliminate any stigma attached to a home that is refitted for accessibility.

Many of the components of universal design are similar to those used for aging-in-place. Here are some of the common features of universal design:

- No steps are used to enter the home.
- Living space, bedrooms, bathrooms, and utilities are on one level.
- Wider doorways and hallways allow for wheelchair passage.
- Extra floor space allows room for turning in a wheelchair.

You can see the many opportunities and challenges that universal design offers for interior designers. This is an area that is sure to grow as more people become aware of the options it offers and choose to make more long-term plans for both themselves and their families.

The ASID offers information on universal design. In addition, the Universal Design Alliance (www.universaldesign.org) is a nonprofit organization that promotes awareness of this growing field. For more information, contact the American Association of Retired Persons at www.aarp.org/families/home_design/universaldesign.

Sustainable Design

Sustainable design, also called *green building*, is a movement to design buildings and interiors that are healthier for inhabitants, operate in a cost efficient manner, conserve energy and water, manage waste efficiently, and use natural materials that have lower environmental impact.

Green building benefits many types of clients, such as those who are environmentally aware, those who are concerned about high energy costs, or even families with health concerns, such as immune system disorders or severe allergic conditions.

The U.S. Green Building Council is collaborating with the ASID Foundation to develop sustainable practice guidelines and educational resources for existing homeowners and residential design professionals, suppliers, and contractors. The goal of this undertaking is to foster home renovation and remodeling practices that minimize impacts on the environment and human health.

Contact the ASID for more information about sustainable design. In addition you may visit the U.S. Green Building Council at www.usgbc.org to learn more about working in this important and growing field.

A Final Thought

As a new interior designer, you will face the challenge of learning from the history of your profession while striving to meet the changing needs of future clients. In order to successfully accomplish this, you will have to maintain the highest standards of design, learn to incorporate environmental arts, and be able to integrate your education with the experience you will gain from each project you work on.

You have learned from reading this book that interior design has four aspects: art, science and technology, profession, and business. The ability to assimilate these four aspects of the profession into your daily work routine will greatly contribute to your success. It's important to remember that you will have a strong and lasting impact on the lives of your clients, particularly if you work in residential design. In short you will be striving to provide a service that makes your clients very happy, and this will in turn lead to your professional success.

Further Reading

Interior Design

Abercrombie, Stanley, and Sherrill Whiton. *Interior Design and Decoration*, 6th ed. Upper Saddle River, N.J.: Prentice Hall, 2006.

Ballast, David Kent. *Interior Design Reference Manual: A Guide to the NCIDQ Exam*, 2nd ed. Belmont, Calif.: Professional Publications, 2002.

Beacham, Cindy V., et al. *Designing YOUR Future: An Introduction to Career Preparation and Professional Practices in Interior Design*. Upper Saddle River, N.J.: Prentice Hall, 2007.

Day, Christopher. *Places of the Soul: Architecture and Environmental Design as a Healing Art*, 2nd ed. Burlington, Mass.: Architectural Press, 2003.

Day, Christopher, and Rosie Parnell. *Consensus Design: Socially Inclusive Process*. Burlington, Mass.: Architectural Press, 2002.

Guthrie, Pat. *Interior Designer's Portable Handbook*. New York: McGraw-Hill Professional Publishing, 2000.

Jackman, Dianne R., et al. *The Guide to Textiles for Interiors*, 3rd ed. Winnipeg, MB: Portage and Main Press, 2003.

Karlen, Mark, and James Benya. *Lighting Design Basics*. New York: Wiley, 2004.

Kirkpatrick, Beverly, and James M. Kirkpatrick. *AutoCAD 2008 for Interior Design & Space Planning*. Upper Saddle River, N.J.: Prentice Hall, 2007.

Knackstedt, Mary V. *The Interior Design Business Handbook: A Complete Guide to Profitability*, 4th ed. New York: Wiley, 2006.

Koenig, Peter A. *Design Graphics: Drawing Techniques for Design Professionals*, 2nd ed. Upper Saddle River, N.J.: Prentice Hall, 2005.

Kopec, David. *Environmental Psychology for Design*. New York: Fairchild Books and Visuals, 2006.

Marcus, Clare C. *House as a Mirror of Self: Exploring the Deeper Meaning of Home*. London: Nicholas-Hays, 2006.

McGowan, Maryrose. *Specifying Interiors: A Guide to Construction and FF&E for Residential and Commercial Interiors Projects*, 2nd ed. New York: Wiley, 2005.

Mitton, Maureen. *Interior Design Visual Presentation: A Guide to Graphics, Models, & Presentation Techniques*, 3rd ed. New York: Wiley, 2007.

Orr, David R. *The Nature of Design: Ecology, Culture, and Human Intention*. New York: Oxford University Press USA, 2002.

Phillips, Nita B., and Suzanne DeWalt. *How to Start a Home-Based Interior Design Business*, 4th ed. Guilford, Conn.: Globe Pequot Press, 2006.

Pile, John F. *Interior Design*, 3rd ed. Upper Saddle River, N.J.: Prentice Hall, 2003.

Piotrowski, Christine M. *Designing Commercial Interiors*, 2nd ed. New York: Wiley, 2007.

———— *Professional Practice for Interior Designers*, 4th ed. New York: Wiley, 2007.

Poore, Jonathan. *Interior Color by Design, Volume 2: A Design Tool for Homeowners, Designers, and Architects*. Gloucester, Mass.: Rockport Publishers, 2005.

Rengel, Roberto J. *Shaping Interior Space*. New York: Fairchild Books and Visuals, 2007.

Riggs, J. Rosemary. *Materials and Components of Interior Architecture*, 7th ed. Upper Saddle River, N.J.: Prentice Hall, 2007.

Schoeser, Mary. *World Textiles: A Concise History*. London: Thames and Hudson, 2003.

Starmer, Anna. *The Color Scheme Bible: Inspirational Palettes for Designing Home Interiors*. London: Quarto Publishing, 2005.

Williams, Theo Stephan. *The Interior Designers Guide to Pricing, Estimating, and Budgeting*. New York: Allworth Press, 2005.

Winchip, Susan M. *Sustainable Design for Interior Environments*. New York: Fairchild Books and Visuals, 2007.

College Applications, Résumés, Cover Letters, and Interviews

Bennett, Scott. *The Elements of Résumé Style: Essential Rules and Eye-Opening Advice for Writing Résumés and Cover Letters That Work*. New York: AMACOM, 2005.

Enelow, Wendy S., and Arnold G. Boldt. *No-Nonsense Cover Letters: The Essential Guide to Creating Attention-Grabbing*

Cover Letters That Get Interviews & Job Offers. Franklin Lakes, N.J.: Career Press, 2007.

Kador, John. *201 Best Questions to Ask on Your Interview.* New York: McGraw-Hill, 2002.

London, Michael, and Stephen Kramer. *The New Rules of College Admissions: Ten Former Admissions Officers Reveal What It Takes to Get into College Today.* New York: Fireside, 2006.

Rankin, Estelle, and Barbara Murphy. *McGraw-Hill's Writing an Outstanding College Application Essay.* New York: McGraw-Hill, 2005.

Simons, Warren, and Rose Curtis. *The Résumé.com Guide to Writing Unbeatable Résumés.* New York: McGraw-Hill, 2004.

Springer, Sally, and Marion R. Franck. *Admission Matters: What Students and Parents Need to Know About Getting into College.* San Francisco: Jossey-Bass, 2005.

Stein, Marky. *Fearless Interviewing: How to Win the Job by Communicating with Confidence.* New York: McGraw-Hill, 2002.